SQUIRE AND PARTNERS

CONTENTS

Regional modernism is derived
from contemporary principles but
is informed by a sense of place

The architectural form responds to the order of the city and how it is understood

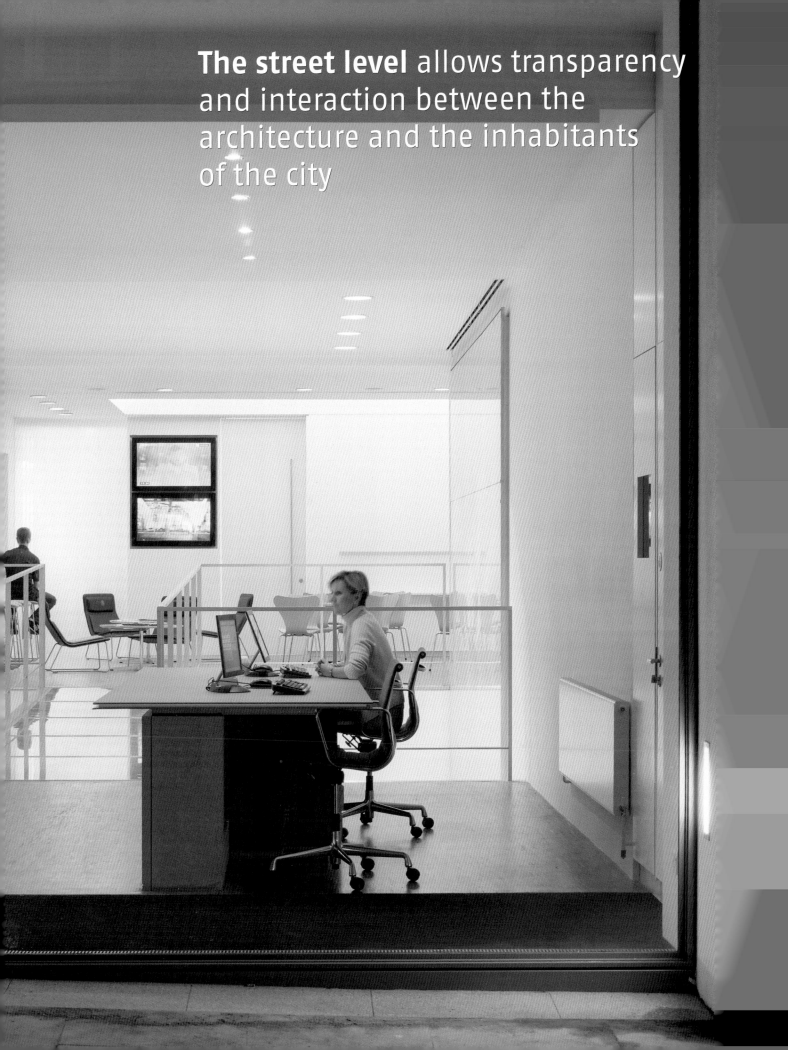

The street level allows transparency and interaction between the architecture and the inhabitants of the city

The urban plane responds to
the rhythm and fabric of the site,
and defines streets and spaces

The sky storey addresses the city as a whole; defining its skyline and its profile

The materials and details give life and resonance to the architectural idea

Space and light are revealed
through the section

Squire and Partners' work is informed by modernist principles but is derived from a sense of place. The practice describes its architecture as regional modernism. Buildings are designed to respond to the underlying themes of materiality, scale and proportion, which are common to the locations in which they are placed. The architecture also responds to the practical circumstances of building in established streetscapes and often in recognized historic areas. Squire and Partners was launched in 1976 by Michael Squire, who is a graduate of the Cambridge department of architecture and the son of the architect Raglan Squire (his grandfather, the New Statesman editor J.C. Squire, founded the influential Architecture Club in the 1920s to encourage dialogue between architects and the press). In the early years, the practice concentrated on interiors and relatively modest refurbishment schemes. It quickly achieved a reputation for sensitivity to place and context and concern for careful detail which have been translated into a wider sphere of practice since the 1980s. Paul Harrison joined Squire and Partners shortly after its inception and brings to the practice a unique understanding of how things are made and technically assembled. Paul was trained at the Leeds School of Architecture, an institution with a reputation for instilling strong professional and management skills into its graduates – his expertise at developing and managing projects from initial concept to completed building is legendary and has contributed greatly to Squire and Partners' reputation for delivering buildable schemes on schedule and to budget.

The architectural scene in the 1980s was confused. For Squire and Partners, neither High-tech, nor American-style Post Modernism, nor, indeed, the revived Classicism favoured by the Prince of Wales, seemed to provide a way forward. The practice began to develop a distinctive approach: regional modernism.

Right: Dunhill Building,
Jermyn Street
Below: Peter Jones,
Sloane Square

From the 1920s to the 1960s modern architecture developed an approach to design that was international and universal – the so-called International Style was the outcome. This was the orthodoxy that prevailed in schools of architecture throughout the 1950s and 1960s. It was decisively challenged by the idea of Critical Regionalism propounded in the Seventies by Kenneth Frampton – for Michael Squire, Frampton's arguments provide an intellectual framework for a modern architecture informed by place. In contrast to the universalism of High-tech, Squire and Partners has developed an architectural language which Michael Squire describes as "rooted in a sense of place and location, while remaining rigorous and rational".

Squire and Partners is a London practice through and through. So far, all of its built work is in London (though it has aspirations beyond London) and much of that is in the City of Westminster, 70% of the territory of which is contained within Conservation Areas.

London is, for all the huge scale and diverse character of its later 19th and 20th century development, very largely a Georgian and a Classical city – the terraced house is, perhaps, the most persistent model for building in the capital, providing it with a grain, an established sense of proportions and a palette of materials (brick, stone and stucco). A constant element, for example, in the Classical tradition is the expression of the first floor as a piano nobile, where the principal living spaces are located. The facade of a Georgian house, from the basement area to the upper storeys (inhabited in the past by servants), is an expression of social hierarchy which has stamped its image on London's streets from Islington to Kennington, from Bow to Belgravia. Until the post-war period, London's commercial architecture reflected a broad consensus on issues like scale and materials. A street such as Jermyn Street, with buildings from the 18th century to the present day, may contain a number of styles, but the result is a harmony because that consensus has always prevailed. "The

London style", as Squire and Partners perceives it, is based on a quality of "London-ness" which is about responding to the character of a city – Squire and Partners' shortlisted 1991 competition scheme for the Museum of Scotland in Edinburgh demonstrated the adaptability of this approach to a very different urban context.

Large modern buildings, regardless of style, employ structural technologies that the Georgians did not possess, notably the load-bearing concrete or steel frame. The essence of the Squire approach is reconciling a modern structure with a skin which is both rational and modern, avoiding the "shams" associated with Post Modernism, and equally urban and contextual. Usually this means clearly expressing the frame as a primary structure which defines the look of a building – modern masters like Terragni and Kahn provide good exemplars for the strongly articulated frame. Within the discipline of the frame, there is scope for great variety of means in creating the enclosure which defines the internal spaces. The skin of a building may be formed of glass, metal, brick, stone or render, with window openings which reflect the use of the spaces they serve, but ignoring the structural frame is alien to the Squire approach. A modern commercial building, however, has a relationship to the street very different from that of the essentially private Georgian house – access and a certain vitality, rather than privacy and discretion, is the aim. Upper floors, with the potential for views and ample natural light, have become primary spaces. So the rhythm and hierarchy of the traditional facade must be re-articulated. Modern technology allows designers to disregard the constraints imposed by the historic loadbearing capacity of compressive structure – for Michael Squire, this underlines the need "to analyse the context and respond to it in a modern way so that contemporary urban architecture remains legible in an historic location". For example, a building like 44-45 Great Marlborough Street evokes the rhythm and proportions

Left: Yale Centre for British Art, New Haven, Connecticut, Louis Kahn
Above: Casa del Fascio, Como, Guiseppe Terragni

of adjacent Victorian buildings without exactly mirroring them. Squire and Partners organise new urban buildings around three distinct elements of their facades, respecting the inherent order of the city. The Street Level allows transparency and interaction between the architecture and the inhabitants of the city. The Urban Plane, incorporating the upper levels of the buildings responds to the rhythm and fabric of the site and defines streets and spaces. The Sky Storey addresses the city as a whole; defining its skyline and its profile, and offering potential which the Georgians or Victorians (in the absence of lifts) could not unlock.

The stylish make-over of 25 Savile Row, essentially a decent 1950s block in need of "lifting", demonstrates what can be achieved at street and roof level. Comparing the new Brook House, with its boldly expressed lower floors of commercial space on Park Lane and floating rooftop penthouse pavilions, with the stodgy 1930s block which it replaced shows how far this sophisticated strategy can improve on more rigidly traditionalist solutions.

Materiality is seen as fundamental to the Squire approach – Carlo Scarpa is, not surprisingly, an influence widely cited by the practice's partners. It is a matter of using the right materials for the location in a rational and appropriate way. The choice of materials reflects a conviction about appropriateness, based on an analysis of the site. At Brook House, for example, stone cladding is used on the side elevations, which adjoin stone-fronted 19th century town houses. At 4 Bouverie Street, Portland stone is used on the principal elevation, which addresses Fleet Street, while brick, contained within metal framed panels, is used on the subsidiary elevations on to secondary streets. The practice's concern for materials is particularly evident in some of its interiors – for example, at 21 Grosvenor Place, where limestone, marble, walnut, leather and steel are brought together to create an effect which is completely modern but with the understated opulence of a London clubhouse.

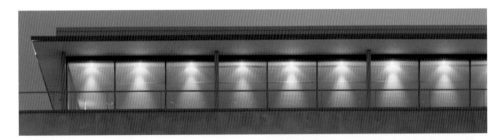

Above: Sky storey,
4 Grosvenor Place
Left: Urban Plane,
111 Strand
Right: Street level,
10 Dean Farrar Street

Left: Vogan's Mill
Below: Sufferance Wharf

Although Westminster has been the principal locale for Squire and Partners' work to date, it has a long record of building in London Docklands. Here the established context found in Belgravia or Mayfair did not apply and the stress was on regeneration. Vogan's Mill in Bermondsey was a redundant silo with a group of listed warehouses attached. The silo was radically rebuilt to form a 17 storey residential tower, a distinctive new Docklands landmark with an extraordinary three storey penthouse on top, while the refurbished warehouses contain 48 apartments. The development was completed in 1989. New buildings in Docklands demanded an appropriate architectural language which reflected some sense of place and history. At Sufferance Wharf on the Isle of Dogs, Squire and Partners' development of apartments and houses, completed in 1990, managed to reflect the scale and robust aesthetic of the typical Docklands warehouse without too many explicit references – and with no trace of the Post Modern detailing seen elsewhere in the area. The development at Sufferance Wharf creates new streets and spaces within the site and by building to the back of existing pavements, reinforces the historic street pattern. This commitment to a legible urban framework responding to the existing grain and infrastructure is important to Squire and Partners' architectural approach, which adheres to a consistent programme from masterplanning large urban areas to detailing specific building elements. The success of the practice's work in Docklands led to a commission from the London Docklands Development Corporation to design a new youth club (to replace a building demolished for the Limehouse Link road). Offices and residential developments formed the bulk of the practice's work through the 1980s and 90s, but it is not willing to be typecast. The Architects' Journal described the Limehouse building (completed in 1995) as "community architecture of the highest order". Strong in form, the building has a toughness appropriate to its location and function but

Right and below:
Limehouse Youth Club

none of the sentimental condescension which has made "community architecture" a suspect quantity. The materials – timber, fairfaced concrete, galvanised steel – are appropriate to the task, but are used to elegant effect.

Squire and Partners' work in Docklands has informed several areas of its wider practice. Firstly, it introduced the office to issues of masterplanning and urban design, an area where it is surely destined to expand its activities. Its achievement in unlocking the potential of West India Quay was considerable. The site was adjacent to Canary Wharf and contained the finest surviving group of warehouses in London, listed Grade I but long disused. In 1996 the LDDC held a developer/architect competition in which the West India Quay Development Company consortium was successful, with Squire and Partners as masterplanners. The aim of the project was to balance the "office city" of Canary Wharf with a mixed use development incorporating retail, leisure, and hotel developments as well as residential accommodation, much of it in the refurbished warehouses. The quayside was brought to life as a popular venue for eating and drinking. Away from the water, the multiplex cinema complex and multi-storey carpark designed by Squire and Partners provided a buffer against the noise of the adjacent main road and Docklands Light Railway as well as addressing perceived local needs. The 12 storey Horizon Building, also designed by Squire and Partners, houses 40 apartments, its cool, glassy aesthetic contrasting with the massive horizontal bulk of the warehouses. The final component in the Squire masterplan is a mixed-use tower currently being detailed and executed by HOK, in line with Squire and Partners' original conceptual design. The new tower addresses the axis of the quayside and the exit from the Limehouse Link road.

For Squire and Partners, as for other practices, Docklands has offered an opportunity to design on a scale and with a boldness not always possible in the traditional heart of

London and to make a decisive impact on the developing form of new quarters. Further masterplanning exercises took place at Millharbour, where Squire and Partners' blueprint for the Millennium Quarter, further developed by EDAW, includes a striking 37 storey mixed-use tower designed by the practice. At Royal Victoria Docks, the Squire masterplan includes two 330 unit residential developments plus retail, hotel and small business accommodation, while the architecture aims to reinforce a sense of urban identity in what has been until recently a remote area of the far East End – Docklands has enough "object buildings". The Docklands experience has fuelled the diversity of Squire and Partners' work in the early years of a new century – projects such as Bankstock Buildings alongside the Regent's Canal in Hoxton (where it is converting a 1920s warehouse as offices and live/work units and adding a new blade building with a double-height public lobby at canalside level), the church and residential development at Short Street, Lambeth, the Whitechurch Lane housing in Spitalfields, and the CityWell project in King's Cross, which addresses the serious problem of homelessness in the area.

Openness to new ideas and a quest for new areas of practice, beyond a solid established client base, has attracted young talents to Squire and Partners. New partners Mark Way, Martin O'Leary, Jeff Brooks and Murray Levinson are all in their 30s and 40s – and the practice has recognized achievement by granting associate status to ten other staff members. The "re-branding" of the firm in 2001, as Squire and Partners, reflects its belief in the team. Experiment and innovation are seen as vital to the firm's future, but it has a stable base in a growing list of regular clients and continues to develop the tradition of regional modernism on which its initial success was founded. Brook House was obviously a landmark in this respect and the process of securing consent to demolish the existing building was lengthy – the generally

Left: 1 Millharbour
Above: Townsend House

disastrous history of post-war development on Park Lane has made planners and public wary of further change. The corner site at 10 Lower Grosvenor Place, for which the client was the Grosvenor Estate and Redrow, was almost equally sensitive – again a warning of past mistakes is provided by the looming grey bulk of Stag Place nearby. The new scheme replaced a coarse late 19th century block which intruded into a block of listed Georgian buildings, in a Conservation Area close to Victoria station. The development, completed in 1995, aims at harmony with its surroundings while eschewing historicist details – it got the firm support of the then Royal Fine Art Commission. Parnell House on Wilton Road, finished two years later, is more rigorously rational, with extremely crisp detailing and a strong, though dignified, street presence. The unrealised mixed-use scheme for Townsend House, Greycoat Place, is a far more expressive design, incorporating large areas of glazed curtain walling (though still contained firmly within the typical Squire frame, in this case clad in limestone). These last three projects, all within the City of Westminster, illustrate the range of expression possible within the framework of a defined design philosophy.

Two major projects of the early 2000s, 199 Knightsbridge and Belgrave House, Buckingham Palace Road, develop the themes of modern, but increasingly less overt, contextualism on a large scale. In both cases, failed developments of the post-war era (of the 1950s and 1970s respectively) are replaced and the new architecture aims to be both commercial and, to a degree, inspirational – lightness, transparency and a stress on fine materials are themes in both schemes. "Lifting the spirits" could be seen as part of the Squire philosophy and a significant element in the practice's workload has been the reinvention of relatively recent buildings which, though adaptable to future needs, lack presence and style as well as modern services. One of Squire and Partners' established clients, Derwent Valley Holdings, has made

Above: 10 Lower Grosvenor Place

Left and below: 25 Savile Row

this sector one of its specialities. The refurbishment of the 1960s block at 4 Grosvenor Place, which Squire and Partners completed for Derwent Valley in 1995, set the pattern for other projects of this kind. The new reception area, with its fully glazed entrance screen framed in bronze, limestone paving and finely crafted wooden panelling, plus carefully chosen furniture, was clearly something of a labour of love and makes an immediate impression on anyone visiting the building (though it accounted for rather less than 10% of the total refurbishment cost). Following the completion of this phase of work on the building, Derwent Valley commissioned the practice to design a new 250 sqm office penthouse at roof level. Set back from the existing building edge and contained within a minimalist roof garden, the addition takes the form of a glazed pavilion distinct in its language from the original Sixties block. Derwent Valley's confidence in Squire and Partners is reflected in its commission to the practice to fit out its own offices as part of the 25 Savile Row project.

Squire and Partners' decision, in 2001, to move its office from South Kensington to a back street in King's Cross – necessitated, in fact, by the growth of the team to over 90 people and the need for larger premises – seemed to reflect a new spirit in the practice. Squire's new base is a former factory, a utilitarian 1930s structure with its upper floors converted to residential use, off the Gray's Inn Road, minutes' walk from the mainline and underground stations. The area is in the throes of regeneration, with the Channel Tunnel Rail Link arriving at St Pancras in 2007, but it still has a hard edge. The move has proved a complete success, not least in terms of staff approval. The new office is well-equipped for the interactive team working which is central to the Squire and Partners ethos, with a cafe, lots of informal meeting areas and a double height space which is the venue for the all-important weekly project review, when members of the practice report on their schemes to the partners: it is usually a lively occasion.

Right and below:
77 Wicklow Street

This space is open not only to the offices, but can equally be glimpsed from the reception area above. The inclusion of a gallery and restaurant within the Wicklow Street scheme, part of the office community but operating independently, is an expression of the firm's hopes to contribute broadly to the regeneration process in King's Cross. As a stylish and beautifully detailed re-creation of a basically functional space, with a particularly assured approach to the use of natural light, the new office has won many plaudits – and inspired several clients to demand something similar.

Squire and Partners remains a London practice, with its finger firmly on the pulse of London's business and social life. It is, however, increasingly less the West End practice it appeared to be a decade or so ago and is looking towards working beyond the constraints of the capital, which is evident in their appointment for the new British Council offices in Kenya and Ethiopia. The firm has succeeded in maintaining its position in the prime office and residential markets while colonising new areas, including masterplanning and urban regeneration. A quarter of a century into its existence, it appears to have the dynamism and optimism of youth and to be looking forward eagerly to new challenges.

Squire and Partners'
offices are designed to
encourage communication
and interaction in
an efficient and open
environment

The reception is connected to the cafe area by a gently ramped glass bridge, with views down into the space where the office's weekly project meetings take place

Design Reviews are the fulcrum of the design process. All projects are reviewed on a regular basis at all stages of their evolution from conception to completion

Bankstock Buildings
42-44 De Beauvoir Crescent, London N1

This mixed-use project, including office, residential and live/work accommodation and combining refurbishment and new-build, illustrates the growing range of Squire and Partners' portfolio and the practice's interest in urban regeneration. The site, alongside the Regent's Canal, close to Kingsland Road, Hoxton, is mostly occupied by a fine 1920s concrete-framed warehouse, designed by Robert Sharpe (better known for his Bluebird Building in Chelsea). Later accretions to the building are being stripped away as part of the refurbishment scheme, with a new two-storey glazed pavilion added at roof level. A slender nine-storey glazed tower forms a forceful new addition to the site and includes a cafe, gallery and other public amenities in a double height space at canal level. The vocabulary of the tower, like that of the rooftop pavilion, counterpoises solid panels clad in stone or lead with sheer glazing. The development makes a major contribution to the renaissance of a currently under-used (and largely inaccessible) stretch of canalside, with shops and cafes to attract the public. Combining conservation and innovative new design, the project respects the history of the site while generating new uses in an area of redundant industry.

The regenerated building with its contemporary additions, provides animation to Regent's Canal towpath

Client
Dorrington Properties plc
Contract Value
£15m
Quantity Surveyor
Jackson Coles
Structural Engineer
Adams Kara Taylor
Services Engineer
Watkins Payne Partnership
Planning Consultant
Hepher Dixon
**Planning Consent
Anticipated**
2002

Belgrave House
Buckingham Palace Road, London SW1

The existing Belgrave House, an undistinguished 1970s block which has stood empty for some years, has been demolished for this new, 32,000 sqm office development yards from Victoria Station. Its replacement exemplifies Squire and Partners' approach to the design of commercial buildings in an established urban context. The steel-framed building is clad in a mix of Portland stone, limestone and glass, with the street elevation clearly expressing the structural grid – organising the facade as a series of 9m bays helps to break down its scale and create a strong rhythm. Fifth and sixth floors are set back, with minimal metal-framed glazing. The entrance bay is emphasised by its greater width and by the addition of a projecting steel and glass canopy. The Grade II listed Chantrey House, an attractive Edwardian building on the corner of Buckingham Palace Road and Eccleston Place, is retained and converted to provide 36 residential units, with retailing at street level – new penthouse apartments offer views across Belgravia to the river.

This scheme derives its distinction from its calm and rational design strategy, combined with the use of high-quality materials. New tree-planting and landscaping greatly improves the public domain on a busy London thoroughfare. The overall effect of the development is regenerative in both commercial and amenity terms.

A new five storey Portland stone-clad frame reinforces the entrance to Belgrave House from Buckingham Palace Road

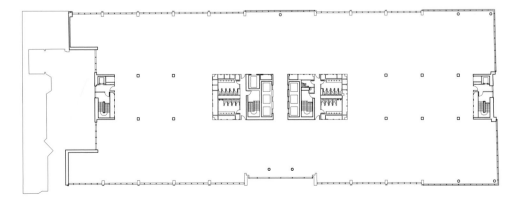

Client
Grosvenor/JER
Contract Value
£58m
Quantity Surveyor
E C Harris
Structural Engineer
Whitby Bird and Partners
Services Engineer
Whitby Bird and Partners
Planning Consultant
Gerald Eve
Main Contractor
Sir Robert McAlpine
Completion
2004

4 Bouverie Street

London EC4

The 2200 sqm office project at Bouverie Street represents a highly contextual, but entirely modern, approach to the redevelopment of a tightly constrained site (within a Conservation Area) at the heart of the former newspaper district around Fleet Street. The seven storey building maximises the potential of the site, contained by Bouverie Street, Pleydell Street and the narrow Lombard Lane, to create highly efficient modern office space.

In practical terms, the scheme was driven by the need to secure flexible, open floor plates with generous natural light – hence the location of the service core alongside the single party wall. The top two floors are set back to protect rights of light in the adjacent streets and to provide an attractive roof terrace with excellent views over the City. The building is entered from Bouverie Street via a ramp or steps – two lifts serve upper floors.

The external facades of the building respond to the context of the surrounding streets and are unified by the overall structural grid, expressed in a Portland stone frame. Portland stone panels are used on the frontage to Bouverie Street, while on the other street elevations the frame is infilled with stack bonded, aluminium-framed brick panels. The street corner is emphasised by a circular bay, fully glazed, an elegant addition to a very varied street scene.

The glass and stone corner on Bouverie and Pleydell Street gives presence to the building when seen from Fleet Street

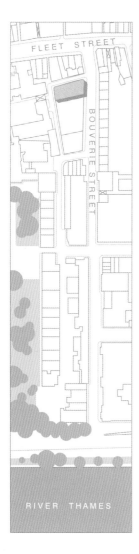

Client
Ebble Trading Ltd
Contract Value
£3.2m
Quantity Surveyor
E C Harris
Structural Engineer
Price and Myers
Services Engineer
Peter Deer and Associates
Main Contractor
Lovell Construction Ltd
Completed
1999

4 BOUVERIE STREET

Planes of Portland
stone set in steel frames
articulate the elevation
to Bouverie Street

The Brand Union
Greencoat House, Francis Street, London SW1

Greencoat House, located behind Victoria Street, was formerly the depository for the nearby Army & Navy stores. It is a stoutly built structure, with a strongly industrial feel – cast iron columns and beams and vaulted concrete soffits define its internal spaces. Squire and Partners' transformation of the building (for client Derwent Valley) has turned it into a working community for small to medium size businesses – many of them media-based – while respecting the original features of the late Victorian structure.

The Brand Union is one of these businesses. Relocating from Soho, the company commissioned Squire and Partners to design its new offices on two floors of Greencoat House (connected by a new stair). The brief was demanding and distinctive. A particular requirement was the provision of informal spaces for meetings and interaction and for social events and entertaining clients. Reception, meeting rooms and cafe are located on the first floor, with offices on the second floor.

The new interventions respond sympathetically to the existing character of the building. First floor spaces are defined by the new stair and the delineating wall linking the reception area to the cafe. The existing ceiling vaults are left exposed, with ventilation and lighting contained in specially designed units. On the second floor, servicing is concentrated within a central spine – which also houses communal facilities such as a coffee point and copying machines and provides a clear order to the working spaces.

A new steel and timber stair connects the two floors which are combined to form a unified working space

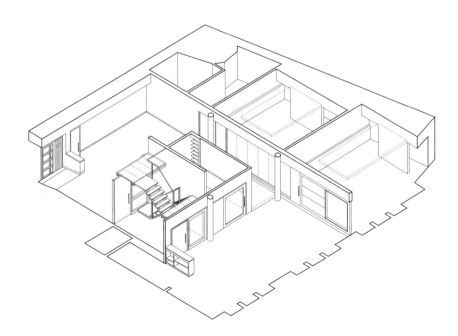

Client
The Brand Union
Contract Value
£0.48m
Quantity Surveyor
E C Harris
Structural Engineer
Price and Myers
Services Engineer
Peter Deer and Associates
Main Contractor
Overbury plc
Completed
1998

'Break-out' and
presentation spaces
are separated by
sliding walls allowing
flexibility

112–120 Brompton Road
14–21 Montpelier Mews
London SW7

Brompton Road is one of London's major shopping streets, linking Knightsbridge with the museums quarter of South Kensington, but is architecturally variegated, with some mundane postwar development. The site for Squire and Partners' scheme is opposite the imposing bulk of Harrod's. The development, located within the Knightsbridge Conservation Area, seeks to respond to the historic scale and character of the area while avoiding obvious historical references. It includes 1000 sqm of retailing at ground and basement levels, with 1700 sqm of offices on three upper floor and two penthouse apartments on the top (fourth) floor. A separate 5 storey residential development faces Montpelier Mews to the rear, with parking below a new landscaped courtyard.

The development is a landmark in the area, demonstrating the potential for new buildings to make a positive contribution to the familiar street scene.

The accommodation stair and glazed passenger lifts rise through a four storey glass fronted volume connecting internal and external circulation

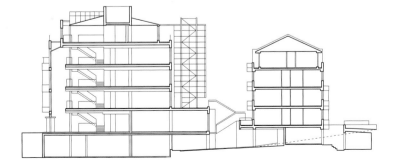

Client
Hightown Holdings Ltd
Contract Value
£8.4m
Quantity Surveyor
E C Harris
Structural Engineer
Alan Baxter and Associates
Services Engineer
M&E Design Services
Main Contractor
McLaughlin and Harvey
Completed
1991

Brook House
Park Lane, London W1

Brook House, completed in 1998, is one of the most prestigious residential developments in London, containing sixteen luxury apartments, with single penthouses occupying the whole of the seventh and eighth floors and commercial space at ground and first floors (plus basement parking). The building is a decisively modern, but appropriately contextual, addition to the eclectic streetscape of Park Lane, where surviving 19th century houses contrast with large-scale hotel, residential and commercial developments constructed from the 1930s on.

Located in a Conservation Area, the development is bounded by streets on three sides – on Woods Mews and Upper Brook Street, the predominant scale remains that of Victorian town houses. The design of the three facades of the building reflects this duality: on Park Lane, the predominant material is self-supporting brick, sitting on a two-storey stone base (which contains the commercial accommodation) and punctuated by stone-clad bays which mark the principal internal spaces. On the side elevations, a stone plane intervenes, stepping down to the scale of the neighbouring houses. The glazed penthouse pavilions which cap the building offer magnificent views of Hyde Park, but also serve to enliven the skyline – Lutyens' pavilions at Grosvenor House provide a precedent.

This finely-crafted building is a bold but dignified addition to the street scene. High quality materials and strongly articulated forms enrich the public domain and provide a model for an urban architecture which is both contemporary and at ease in an historic setting.

The building is a decisively modern, but appropriately contextual, addition to the eclectic streetscape of Park Lane

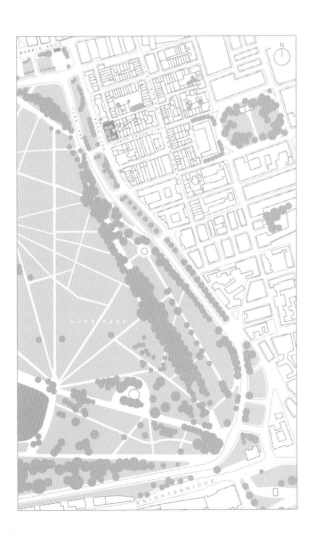

Client
Brook House
Developments Ltd
Contract Value
£20m
Quantity Surveyor
Gibb Ltd
Structural Engineer
Gibb Ltd
Services Engineer
Gibb Ltd
Main Contractor
Higgs and Hill Southern
Completed
1998

A private entrance and
driveway at the rear of
the building allow access
to the entrance hall

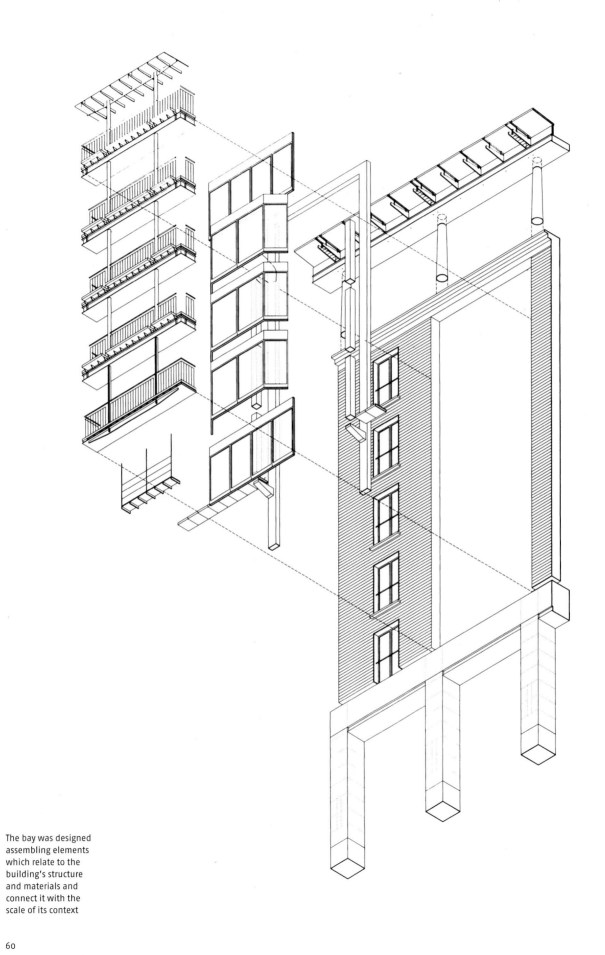

The bay was designed
assembling elements
which relate to the
building's structure
and materials and
connect it with the
scale of its context

Cadogan Pier
Chelsea Embankment, London SW3

Houseboats are a familiar feature of the stretch of the Thames which separates Chelsea and Battersea, but Squire and Partners' Cadogan Pier project is unique in adapting an existing boat hull for use as offices. The brief from client Boultbee Land was to create office space for 10 employees, plus a small sleeping quarter.

The location is alongside Albert Bridge and offers fine views along the river to Battersea Park and Battersea Power Station. The new offices are contained within a new prefabricated steel framed container, with full height glazing on all sides – sliding screens control glare from the water. The curving steel roof has a distinctly nautical look.

The office space includes a raised meeting area and a lowered central office space seating eight people, with two cellular offices for directors. Sleeping area, storage, kitchen and plant are housed at lower deck level, with circular porthole windows providing daylight and reinforcing the nautical ethos. The theme is continued by the finely detailed timber ramp, with metal balustrade, which connects to the pier and provides access to the offices.

A full height glazed enclosure allows views over the river and the park

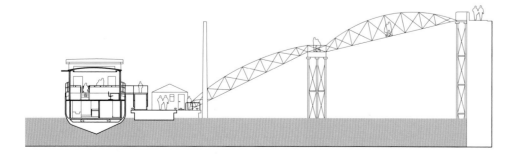

Client
Boultbee Land plc
Planning consent
2000

Chelsea College
King's Road, London SW3

The transformation of a 1960s complex, formerly occupied by Chelsea College, on King's Road, Chelsea, illustrates Squire and Partners' approach to recycling and "lifting" unremarkable, if basically sound, modern buildings. Following a merger with King's College, London, most of the college's accommodation has become redundant, though the high-rise Lightfoot Hall has been retained as student accommodation and extensively refurbished.

The adjacent refectory and student union block, College House, has been radically remodelled as high-quality retail and office space, with the structure stripped down, internally reconstructed and given an attractive new public face. One imperative of the scheme was to achieve a more sympathetic response to the adjacent listed houses on Carlyle Square. The robust, two-storey, limestone clad base, in scale with the square, contains retail space at basement, ground and first floor levels. Two floors of offices above are conceived as a glazed lightweight pavilion, set back from the street line – floor to ceiling glazing is set within bronze frames. A new double-height entrance hall, framed in limestone, set between College House and Lightfoot Hall, serves the offices.

The development combines a mix of uses with a focus on quality appropriate to the King's Road and now provides a confident modern intervention into the period townscape of Chelsea.

A light, glazed two storey pavilion is added to the existing building

Client
Moonstone Properties Ltd
Contract Value
£4m
Project Manager
Delta Property Services Ltd
Quantity Surveyor
E C Harris
Structural Engineer
Price and Myers
Services Engineer
Interserve
Main Contractor
Kajima
Completed
2001

The new entrance glows
at night and reinforces the
connection to Kings Road

CityWell
London NW1

The CityWell development in King's Cross represents a radical new departure for housing in London. Squire and Partners' designs reflect this with a building that has real elegance and a sense of place, while responding efficiently to a highly practical brief.

Developed by a consortium of Crisis, the King's Fund and the London & Quadrant Housing Trust, CityWell provides homes for both key workers (for example, nurses, teachers, catering staff and transport employees) and for homeless people and aims to break down all the social divisions of the housing market.

Architecturally, the aim is to create a memorable development that expresses the clients' ambitions — to make a healthy living environment and contribute to the regeneration of the surrounding area. Public spaces, plus support spaces for residents, break the mould of social housing and the provision of lettable commercial space underpins the scheme financially.

The CityWell tower will act as a landmark connecting the inhabitants with the city outside.

Client
CityWell
Contract Value
£30m
Quantity Surveyor
E C Harris
Structural Engineers
Whitby Bird & Partners
Services Engineer
Fulcrum
Completion
2005

Competitions

Participating in competitions has been an important part of the culture of Squire and Partners for some years. Apart from securing jobs, the competition process is significant to the life of the office, encouraging innovation, the exploration of unfamiliar contexts and creative team working.

Waterloo Vistor Centre Competition For the battlefield of Waterloo in Belgium the practice submitted ideas for a museum and visitor centre. The new building would stand inside a mound created by the demolition of the strategic ridge which formed the main focus of the battle.

It was intended to capitalise on the existing features of the site, with square enclosures echoing the form of the infantry "squares" used at Waterloo. Inside, viewing spaces would spiral to a viewing gallery at the top, where there could be access to a terrace leading on to the field of battle.

Brighton West Pier Competition Squire and Partners' design proposal and feasibility study for Brighton West Pier was prepared for the Brighton West Pier Trust in 1997 and formed the basis for a grant application for Lottery

funding to refurbish and restore the long-derelict listed pier as a prime tourist attraction. The designs provide for mixed use spaces, creating changeable facades which respond to changing seasons and activities along the sea front.

National Museum of Scotland Competition
The shortlisted competition scheme for the Museum of Scotland, Edinburgh – one of six finalists – provided for an extension to the splendid 19th century museum building in Chambers Street. The connection between the two buildings is achieved by means of a ramp enclosed within a glazed screen – a link, but also marking a point of transition from old to new. The arrangement of the new building, three galleries surrounded by narrow alleys containing the vertical circulation, provides a memory of the closes of old Edinburgh.

Blackpool Wind Shelter Competition The wind shelter is made up of three curved blades which, when arranges in the principal formation, create an areodynamic enclosure set on a circular deck which turns on a ball-bearing joint to respond to the wind direction. In the summer it is possible to open the blades into the "wind catcher" mode to allow the seating to catch the breeze and to enjoy a greater aspect and view. The third adjustment of the blades turns the shelter into its "wind waltzer" mode where the wind generates a gentle rotation of the deck which will add another dimension to the experience of the view from the promenade.

44-45 Great Marlborough Street
London W1

The site at Great Marlborough Street is within the Soho Conservation Area and consent to demolish the existing, undistinguished Victorian buildings there was initially refused by Westminster Council. A planning appeal was submitted, with the Commission for Architecture and the Built Environment praising Squire and Partners' proposed replacement for "its clarity and careful attention to the rhythm and detailed treatment of the front elevation". The appeal was allowed in April, 2001, with the inspector ruling that the scheme "would provide a building of subtle quality".

The development vividly illustrates Squire and Partners' approach to "regional modernism", the design of contemporary buildings which respond strongly to their context. The quality of the new building derives from its scale, proportion and materials (Portland stone is the primary cladding material), which reflect the established character of the area – the architectural language of the building is, however, completely modern. The development, containing 2500 sqm of office space, with restaurant use at ground and lower ground levels, contributes positively to the character of the area in visual and commercial terms.

The rhythm of the new building responds to the character of the existing street

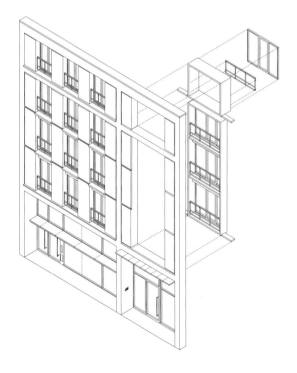

Client
The Apperly Estates Ltd
Contract Value
£4.3m
Quantity Surveyor
Wicksteeds
Structural Engineer
Price and Myers
Services Engineer
Mecserve plc
Main Contractor
Kier London Ltd
Completion
2003

Greencoat House
Francis Street, London SW1

The imposing, late Victorian Greencoat House (originally a depository for the nearby Army & Navy Stores) had been spoiled internally by random alterations and subdivision when Squire and Partners' client, Derwent Valley, acquired the 6 storey building. The brief to the architects was to reinstate its internal quality and unity, defined by the clear structural order of cast iron columns, steel beams and concrete arches, while creating modern office accommodation in the form of suites for small and medium sized companies. A spacious new entrance area was required, along with clear circulation routes within the building, while there was obvious scope for new office accommodation at roof level.

The project was driven not only by a demanding practical brief but by the desire to restore and enhance the building, with new interventions in sympathy with the historic fabric in terms of details and materials (though clearly identifiable as modern additions).

Perhaps the most dramatic transformation was achieved in the entrance area, where the lowering of the flight of steps and addition of a ramp, with the floor level of the entrance hall also lowered, addressed the problems of access. Inside, the existing, highly impressive Victorian cast iron staircase became the focus of the reorganised and enlarged reception area. Two new lifts replaced the existing lift. The conversion of former loading bays into offices and showrooms has animated the ground floor and created a greatly improved connection to the street.

The new entrance provides a transparency which reinforces the connection between the building and the street

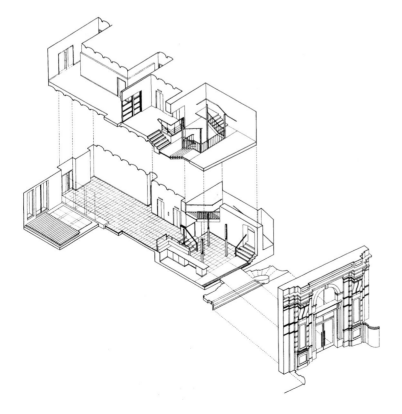

Client
Derwent Valley
Holdings plc
Contract Value
£1.3m
Quantity Surveyor
E C Harris
Structural Engineer
Price and Myers
Services Engineer
Peter Deer and
Associates
Main Contractor
Sames plc
Completed
1997

The existing loading
bays have been
converted to office
accomodation

Greencoat House, 5th floor
Francis Street, London SW1

The new penthouse floor added to Greencoat House, Victoria, formed the final phase of the refurbishment project carried out for client Derwent Valley. The existing rooftop space, which was demolished, was contained within a mansard roof of poor quality, with limited views and low ceilings. The new accommodation has a ceiling height of 3m, with full-height glazing offering spectacular views over Westminster.

The new lightweight structure retains the rhythm of the Victorian building, with solid timber panels set within the glazed envelope and articulating the scale of the internal space. A raised floor, containing air conditioning ducts, allows views across the existing roof parapet. Placing services at floor level allows roof soffits to be of plain plaster, with recessed lighting.

The new penthouse 'sky storey' allows a connection to the city as a whole

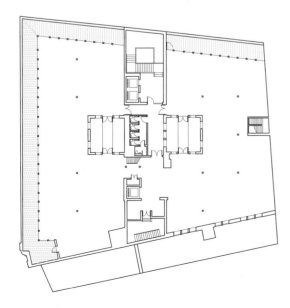

Client
Derwent Valley Holdings plc
Contract Value
£2.3m
Quantity Surveyor
E C Harris
Structural Engineer
Price and Myers
Services Engineer
Peter Deer and Associates
Main Contractor
Interior plc
Completed
2000

6 Greencoat Place
London SW1

Squire and Partners' refurbishment of 6 Greencoat Place – a Victorian depository damaged by wartime bombing and partly rebuilt in the 1950s – focused on the sympathetic reinstatement and updating of the surviving ground and basement levels, where cast iron columns and beams and vaulted ceilings define the character of the interior spaces. These elements have been retained and, where possible, left exposed, in the refurbishment, juxtaposed against new finishes in smooth white plasterboard, metal, timber and limestone.

A new reception area was created in a former loading bay. The removal of an existing lift shaft allowed the frontage to Greencoat Place to be opened up with a new glazed enclosure. Circulation has been improved by inserting a new staircase, naturally lit from above, with views on to the street. Two new lifts, inserted in an existing shaft, are detailed to reflect the industrial character of the building. The reception area is finished in limestone and English oak. Office floors have generous floor to ceiling heights, with the original vaulted ceilings exposed and services placed in a 380mm raised floor.

The cast glass panels in the entrance screen allow a diffused view of the structure behind

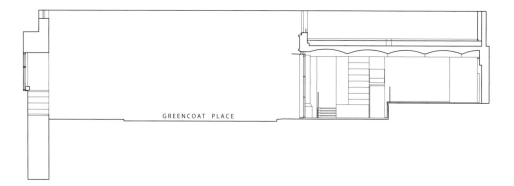

GREENCOAT PLACE

Client
Derwent Valley
Holdings plc
Contract Value
£1.97m
Quantity Surveyor
Davis Langdon and Everest
Structural Engineer
Price and Myers
Services Engineer
Peter Deer and
Associates
Main Contractor
Sames plc
Completed
2001

4 Grosvenor Place
London SW1

The office building at 4 Grosvenor Place occupies a prominent site at the junction of Hyde Park Corner and Halkin Street. Previously rundown and under-valued, it has been vastly enhanced, in both visual and commercial terms, by Squire and Partners' incremental refurbishment project, carried out for client Derwent Valley Holdings.

The original 8 storey building was completed in 1963 to designs by T.P.Bennett – it is a dignified, if austere, structure, clad in smooth Portland stone. Its qualities had been obscured by multiple occupation and random alterations – the building lacked the prestige and presence which its location demanded.

The initial client brief was to improve the entrance and other common areas – the existing recessed entrance was far from prominent and led to a cramped reception area. The new entrance hall is seen as the key transitional space in the heart of the building, providing a strong sense of arrival. The entrance area was extended to the line of the main facade, with minimally detailed glazing set within a bronze frame. Limestone paving extends through the glazed screen to link the interior and exterior of the building. Lighting has been dramatically upgraded, so that the reception area, with its crisp white walls and richly textured elm panelling, is a beacon by night.

Since the completion of this phase of works in 1996, Squire and Partners has completed the new 6th floor penthouse and also carried out fitouts for a number of the tenants within the building.

The existing building is animated and given vitality by the introduction of a new entrance hall at street level

Client
Derwent Valley
Holdings plc
Contract Value Entrance
£0.35m
**Contract Value Office
Interiors**
£4.2m
Structural Engineer
Price and Myers
Services Engineer
Nicholas Wedgwood
Engineers
Main Contractor
Sames plc
Completed
1995

The connection between
the building and Hyde
Park Corner is reinforced
by the new transparency
at street level

4 Grosvenor Place, 6th floor
London SW1

The upper floors of London buildings, even those of comparatively recent date, have often been underused, yet they frequently offer the potential to create outstanding working spaces with remarkable views. At 4 Grosvenor Place, following the completion of earlier refurbishment work for client Derwent Valley, Squire and Partners added a new penthouse level containing 250 sqm of office accommodation linked by a new steel and timber staircase to the existing 5th floor.

The relative severity of the 1960s block on which it is set enhances the impact of the new, lightweight glass and steel pavilion, with its fully glazed transparent frontage to Halkin Street. A solid bridging element, connecting it to the existing lifts and core of the building, is discreetly clad in Portland stone to match the Sixties work.

The structural columns within the new offices are taken beyond the glazed facade to free the space within, while the steel transfer structure below is overlaid with timber decking to create an attractive external deck. The aim is to break down the division between exterior and interior and create a pleasant break-out space for fine summer days.

A new 'sky storey' creates added value and connects the buildings to the city as a whole

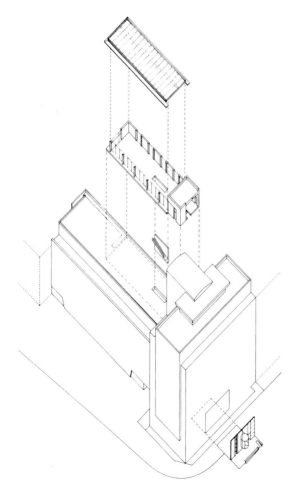

Client
Derwent Valley Holdings plc
Contract Value
£0.5m
Quantity Surveyor
Davis Langdon and Everest
Structural Engineers
Price and Myers
Services Engineer
Peter Deer and Associates
Main Contractor
Sames plc
Completed
1998

21 Grosvenor Place
London SW1

The new reception area and office refurbishment at 21 Grosvenor Place is one of a number of projects in which Squire and Partners has enhanced and upgraded existing commercial buildings, in this case a 1930s block, formerly known as Iron Trades House.

The existing building is a dignified (though unlisted) structure, Classical in style. Westminster planners were anxious to maintain its external integrity as part of the refurbishment programme. Two retained stone porticoes frame the new reception area, set behind a fully glazed facade framed in stainless steel.

Inside the reception space, white walls and limestone floors provide a clean and crisp look, with warmth and texture infused by the walnut veneered lift wall and black leather-clad reception desk, with a single panel of fine marble facing the street. An original steel column has been retained, as a reference to the original associations of the building, and acts as a sculptural focus for the space. The backdrop is provided by a wall faced in Portland stone.

The project included the complete refurbishment of four floors of offices, while the top two floors, occupied by the French Embassy, have had their common spaces overhauled to match the standard of the other floors. The entire project was completed within a 12 month construction programme.

Materials and details give life and resonance to the architectural idea

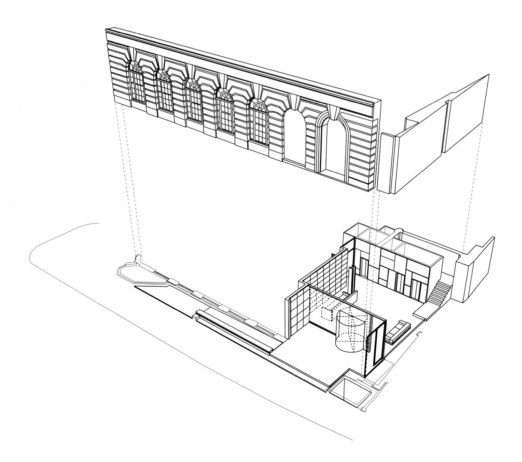

Client
Derwent Valley
Holdings plc
Contract Value
£6.2m
Quantity Surveyor
Davis Langdon and Everest
Structural Engineer
Price and Myers
Services Engineer
Cundall Johnston and
Partners
Main Contractor
Sames plc
Completed
2002

The layering of a new glazed screen behind the existing stone facade provides a transitional area at the threshold

Horizon Building, West India Quay
London E14

Squire and Partners' Horizon Building at West India Quay is an elegant 12 storey residential tower which forms an integral part of the mixed use masterplan for the area. The building forms the northern boundary of a new public square and contains 40 apartments, including four duplex units and a penthouse with dramatic views over Docklands and City. Two retail units are provided at ground floor level.

The architectural language is designed to complement and contrast with that of the nearby Grade I listed warehouses. A limestone clad frame encloses a steel framed, double glazed window system, carefully detailed and offering all residents superb views of the new square and dock.

The cantilevered balconies articulate the facade

Horizon Building, West India Quay

Client
St George North London
Contract Value
£4m
Quantity Surveyor
E C Harris
Structural Engineer
Waterman Partnership
Main Contractor
St George North London
Completed
2000

The Hurlingham Club, New Visitor Facilities
Fulham, London SW6

In the second phase of work at the historic Hurlingham Club in Fulham a new function suite, including ballroom, theatre, servery and dining rooms, is being created, with accommodation for up to 800 guests. The emphasis in the scheme is on flexibility, in order to cater for a wide range of events. Offices for the club are provided at first floor level.

A key issue in the design of the new addition is that of style. Working in consultation with English Heritage, Squire and Partners has developed a language for the new work which refers to the style of the Georgian era without copying it. Limestone pilasters give the elevation of the new building a strong rhythm, with full height glazed doors providing access to the lawns. A 10m high fitted glass and steel dome marks the entrance to the function area. A barrel-vaulted glass ceiling extends along the entire length of the new Palm Court, providing ample natural light inside.

The new function rooms are lit by a glazed dome and address the croquet lawns and the river beyond

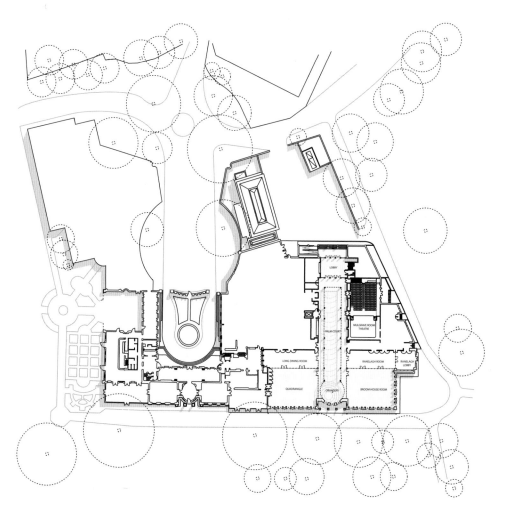

Client
The Hurlingham Club
Contract Value
£12.5m
Quantity Surveyor
E C Harris
Structural Engineer
Whitby Bird and Partners
Services Engineer
Halcrow
Main Contractor
M J Gleeson Group plc
Completion
2004

The palm court is used
as a club room and bar
as well as part of the
main function spaces

The Hurlingham Club, Gymnasium
Fulham, London SW6

The Hurlingham Club, established in 1869, is one of the most famous sporting centres in the world and the venue for major events in the world of tennis, croquet and bowls as well as many prestigious social gatherings. It occupies the Grade II* listed late Georgian Hurlingham House in Fulham, which was extended by Lutyens in the 1900s. Squire and Partners' phased programme of work at the club increases its range of facilities while respecting the character of the existing buildings and their parkland setting.

The first phase of work provided a state-of-the-art gymnasium (extending an existing fitness centre) on two floors, linked by a central daylit void. The style of the new building was carefully chosen to complement the adjacent listed buildings without resorting to pastiche. Traditional timber windows and doors and a lead roof reflect this stress on continuity. The toplit entrance lobby, floored in grey limestone, connects the new car park to Four in Hand Yard.

The well equipped gymnasium is located on two floors, linked by a central daylit void

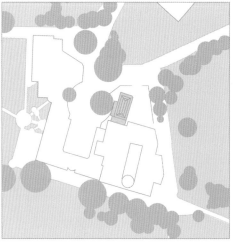

Client
The Hurlingham Club
Contract Value
£2.5m
Quantity Surveyor
E C Harris
Structural Engineer
Whitby Bird and Partners
Services Engineer
Halcrow
Main Contractor
R Durtnell and Sons
Completed
2001

The Knightsbridge
199 Knightsbridge, London SW7

Squire and Partners' Knightsbridge development replaces a dull and intrusive 1950s office block which paradoxically occupied one of the finest sites in London, close to fashionable Knightsbridge, Harrods and Hyde Park. In developing the project, which provides 205 new residential units, the architects addressed complex issues of scale and context – the site is flanked, on one side, by the bulky Normandie Hotel, on the other by listed Georgian terraces – the Sixties Knightsbridge Barracks is across the road.

The new building is a confident, even expansive, example of contemporary design which pays regard to the Classically-rooted "London style" in terms of its strong composition and modelling and the assured rhythm of its facades. A two storey base supports the six floors contained within the main limestone-clad frame, which contains full height glazing panels within an 11.5m grid – two upper floors are expressed as a glazed rooftop pavilion, with two-storey penthouse pavilions punctuating the skyline. The central section of the elevation is further articulated by recessing the second to seventh floors to provide open balconies.

Squire and Partners' strategy was to break down the development into two distinct blocks, with the lower western block, stepping down to Trevor Street, partly clad in brick in a more solid fashion than the main block.

A tranquil landscaped square has been formed to the rear of the site, flanked by maisonettes – it is laid out in a formal manner, with areas of hard and soft landscaping, clipped trees and a central reflecting pool.

The project demonstrates the potential for high quality, entirely contemporary modern residential design in central London – it sets a new standard for luxury living.

Broken down into two distinct buildings the new design brings animation at street level and outlook from the 'sky storey' pavilions

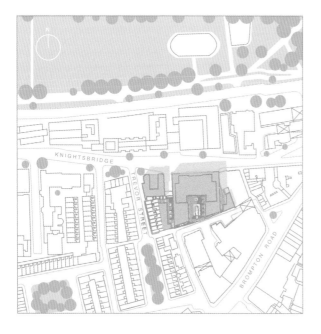

Client
199 Knightsbridge Development Ltd
Contract Value
£130m
Project Manager
199 Knightsbridge Project Management
Quantity Surveyor
Gardiner and Theobald
Structural Engineer
WSP
Services Engineer
WSP
Planning consultant
GVA Grimley
Main Contractor
Multiplex Constructions Pty Ltd
Completion
2004

A new landscaped
courtyard responds
to the adjacent
traditional London
squares, and is seen
from the entrance hall

Limehouse Youth Club
Limehouse Causeway, London E14

The new Limehouse Youth Club replaced a building demolished as part of the Limehouse Link road project. Squire and Partners was commissioned by the London Docklands Development Corporation to design a replacement on a site at Limehouse Causeway. Functional issues apart – the brief called for a variety of spaces for sports and other activities – the client sought a memorable building with landmark qualities, constructed of high quality materials. A bold statement was needed, since the context was highly variegated – the towers of Canary Wharf form a backdrop while the immediate surroundings are far more modest in scale.

The central, 20m x 12m multi-purpose hall became the focus of the design, with ancillary spaces arranged in vaulted areas around the perimeter – a strong diagram which reflects the need for flexibility and the potential to rent out areas to outside organisations.

This is a large and prominent building which gives new substance to the idea of "community architecture". Its materials are selected for hard wear – brick, timber cladding, mill-finished aluminium, galvanised windows and fair-faced concrete columns. Inside, the use of bold colour and generous natural light produces spaces which are dynamic and inspirational as well as practical.

The Architects' Journal described the Limehouse building as "community architecture of the highest order".

The materials are appropriate to the task, but are used to elegant effect

Client
London Docklands
Development Corporation
Contract Value
£1.1m
Quantity Surveyor
E C Harris
Structural Engineer
TZG Partnership
Services Engineer
JMS Associates
Main Contractor
J Hodgson
Completed
1995

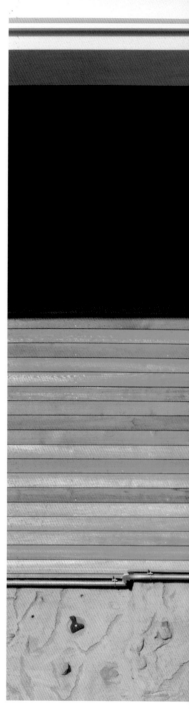

The climbing wall provides both an activity for members of the youth club and funding through sub-letting in the evenings

The East End and Docklands has formed a major focus for Squire and Partners' work over more than a decade. The practice's usual interest in context and locale has been particularly stimulated by working in the extensive region of London. The local building heritage includes a strong industrial and maritime element, seen in surviving factory and warehouse buildings, now mostly adapted to alternative uses. The practice has sought to develop an appropriate mode of new design which reflects this tradition.

Chinnocks Wharf in Narrow Street, is a development of 38 apartments adjacent to the Limehouse Basin entrance, designed for developer St George, responding to the river-side setting with a strong composition, realised in traditional stock brick and render, which has an appropriate scale and toughness.
Client St George North London

Greenwich View Place overlooking Millwall Outer Dock in the Isle of Dogs, is a 116 unit residential development which replaces an existing industrial complex. Again, the architectural vocabulary is firmly contemporary, with crisp detailing – light steel balustrades, white render, timber screens with projecting balconies. The composition roots the building firmly in the site, with a two-level duplex arcade acting as the base and the top articulated as a series of light-weight pavilions. A central garden provides an internal focus for the development.
Client Ballymore Properties

Royal Victoria Docks
Squire and Partners gained planning consent in 2001 for the first of two 330 unit residential developments, with ancillary small business and retail uses, alongside the Royal Victoria Dock. The project is in accord with Squire and Partners' approved masterplan for the area. The project makes a strong response to the east–west axis of the Royal Docks, being organised in five linear blocks, three of which directly address the dockside. A second layer of accommodation provides an animated streetscape reinforcing the axis to the nearby ExCeL exhibition centre.
Client Barratt (East London) Ltd

16–32 Whitechurch Lane in Whitechapel required the practice to work within the constraints of an extant planning consent which dictated the massing of the new housing development. Nonetheless, the completed scheme reflects the considerable care given to detailing and the choice of materials. The site adjoins an area of industry to the south, so that the apartments have living spaces overlooking parkland to the north. The use of simple and solid materials – engineering brick, perforated metal, render and timber – echoes the industrial traditions of the area.
Client Ballymore Properties

90 Long Acre
London WC2

This scheme addressed the practical deficiencies and poor public image of an office development at the heart of Covent Garden, designed by Richard Seifert and Partners in the 1970s and with a potentially long lifespan – but in need of an element of refurbishment and re-branding.

The entrance via an external raised piazza on Long Acre was uninviting and detached from the street – the piazza itself was a tired and claustrophobic area while the reception area was low and poorly lit. Squire and Partners was asked to re-evaluate both, as well as refurbishing some 5,600 sqm of office space on five floors vacated by a departing tenant. The client wished to give the building a new image and culture more appropriate to its location.

The new double-height reception area has been formed by removing part of the first floor slab, with a simple palette of materials (white plaster, white marble, limestone, timber and stainless steel) used to create an elegant and luminous interior. The piazza has been totally recast, with granite paving, raised planters, low Portland stone walls and appropriate planting to make an inviting preface to the building.

The landscaped space at the front of 90 Long Acre connects the building to Covent Garden as a whole

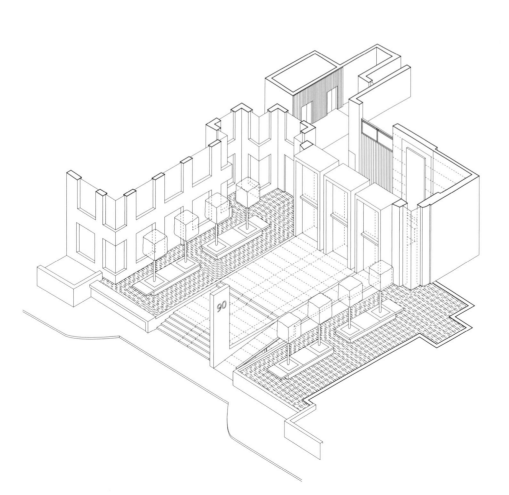

Client
MEPC UK Ltd and Asticus (UK) Ltd
Contract Value
£6m
Project Manager
E C Harris
Quantity Surveyor
E C Harris
Structural Engineer
Price and Myers
Services Engineer
Mecserve
Main Contractor
Overbury
Completed
1998

10 Lower Grosvenor Place
London SW1

The issue of context was critical in this 2000 sqm office development close to Victoria Station, designed for the Grosvenor Estate and Redrow. The development replaced an 1860s residential block, Ranelagh House, on the corner of Lower Grosvenor Place and Beeston Place. The buildings to either side, of early Victorian date, are listed and faced in magnolia-coloured stucco, like the houses in nearby Victoria Square. The unlisted, brick built Victorian block was a brash intruder and its demolition was relatively uncontroversial.

Squire and Partners' five-storey replacement is designed to relate closely to the adjacent terraces while avoiding historicist pastiche and is a subtle exercise in contextual design. The basic diagram of the facades echoes the Classical divisions of base, piano nobile and attics, echoing the rhythm of neighbouring buildings. At fourth floor level, however, where the building steps back, the elevation is given an entirely contemporary form, with a lightweight steel and glass pavilion providing excellent office space with fine views out. The glazed screen appears to extend behind the main facade, which is rendered to match the adjoining terraces. Plant is located at basement level to leave the roof level clear.

The most prominent external feature of the building is the glazed rotunda which marks the street corner. This is again a reinterpretation of a historic feature, seen in many of London's Georgian and Victorian streets, but achieved in a contemporary manner and providing the scheme with a powerful marker.

At 10 Lower Grosvenor Place the 'urban plane' responds to the rhythm and fabric of adjoining buildings

Client
Grosvenor Redrow in Partnership
Contract Value
£3.7m
Quantity Surveyor
E C Harris
Structural Engineer
Cameron Taylor Bedford
Services Engineer
Foremans
Main Contractor
Laing Construction
Completed
1999

The new building
responds to the
adjoining Grade II'
listed building
and completes the
urban block

1 Millharbour
London E14

Squire and Partners' mixed-use tower at 1 Millharbour, next to South Quay station in Docklands, forms a focus for the continued development of the "Millennium Quarter", close to Millwall Dock and adjacent to the spectacularly successful Canary Wharf office city.

The practice collaborated with EDAW on the development of the initial masterplan for the Millennium Quarter, with the tower seen as a prime focus for regeneration and growth. The designs took their cue from Canary Wharf in terms of their boldness of concept and close attention to detail.

The design of the tower (initially 37 storeys, later reduced to 25) consists of two highly glazed, transparent wings separated by a central, stone-clad core. The office floors take the form of "villages", served by sky gardens which act as social spaces. A public viewing gallery at roof level will offer spectacular views across London.

The new public square proposed at ground level is central to the scheme and is seen as the natural centre of this area of Docklands, maximising public use of the waterfront and injecting new vitality into the area. The lower levels of the tower contain restaurant and retail space acting as an extension of the public domain.

The tower consists of two separate blades connected to a central core which terminates in a glazed viewing gallery

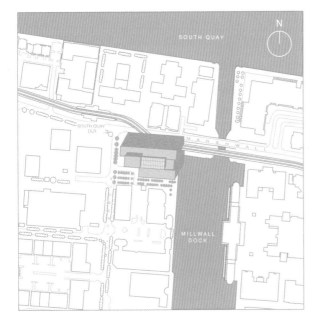

Client
Ballymore Properties
Contract Value
£200m
Quantity Surveyor
Davis Langdon and Everest
Structural Engineer
Ove Arup and Partners
Services Engineer
Roger Preston and
Partners
Main Contractor
Ballymore Commercial
**Original Planning
Application**
1999

A new floating market and
boating platform connects
the tower to the dock

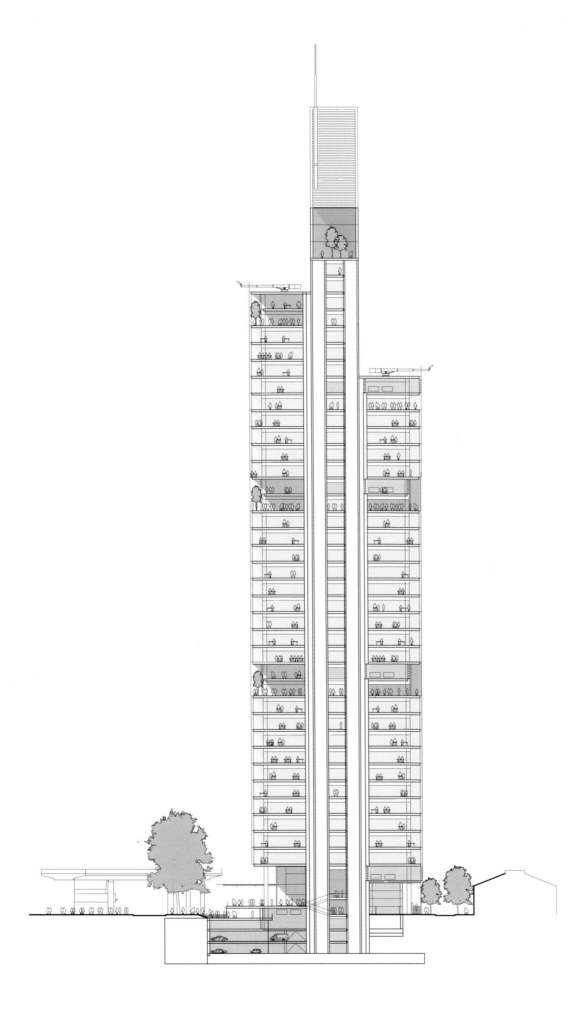

The entrance hall and reception area of an office building, whether old or new, has a key role in establishing the image and culture of the building. The reconstruction of entrance and reception areas has formed a key component in many of the office refurbishment schemes carried out by Squire and Partners.

10 Dean Farrar Street is a brick clad building dating from 1982. Squire and Partners was commissioned to enhance the entrance hall, lift lobby and WCs. An existing heavy canopy was removed and the clear glazed screen to the entrance hall brought forward under a new lightweight canopy to give the building more presence on the street and create an open sense of transition from pavement to interior. The materials used inside – timber, plaster and limestone – create a warm and welcoming effect.
Client Derwent Valley Holdings plc

101 Finsbury Pavement The refurbishment of the early eighties block at 101 Finsbury pavement has significantly upgraded the office spaces (totalling nearly 5,500 sqm) on the ground to fourth floors of the building, while providing a striking new reception area which gives it a new and more inviting public face. The reception area of the building was previously dark and confusing, with a disconcertingly narrow entrance and poor signage. The new entrance area is a double height space finished in white plaster, with a limestone floor inlaid with stainless steel.
Client MEPC and P&O Developments

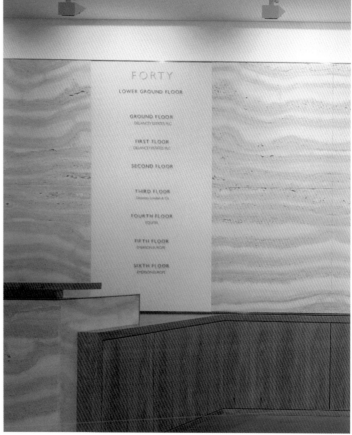

Gordon House is a former 1920's depository building, reconfigured with a new entrance befitting the scale and location of the building, and office accommodation above. The design of the new entrance, reception and tenancies responds to and compliments the original features of the industrial building such as the vaulted concrete soffits and exposed cast iron structure. A series of new perforated screens create layers through which the new entrance is revealed. Concrete, terrazzo, steel and render are the robust palette of materials used, softened and modelled by sculptural lighting set within the fabric of walls and windows.
Client Derwent Valley Central

40 Portman Square Squire and Partners refurbished the entire building for client Delancey Estates plc, which located its own offices on the first floor. The redesign of the entrance area included the addition of a new lightweight canopy externally, with travertine, basalt stone and elm used to dramatic effect in the fit-out.
Client Delancey Estates plc

Squire and Partners' expertise in the design of office interiors reflects the practice's keen interest in natural lighting, the integration of technology into buildings and the appropriate use of materials as well as its innovative approach to space planning and the creation of places which encourage interaction and teamworking. The practice also has a strong reputation for making offices with a dynamic public image, not least through the inclusion of well-designed and memorable reception areas.

Derwent Valley Holdings Squire and Partners designed new offices for this long standing client in the building which it had refurbished for them at 25 Savile Row. The close collaborative relationship between the two companies informed the design process. The aim was to create a distinct identity that reflected the client's reputation for commissioning high quality modern design.

The office space includes a reception area at 4th floor level, connected to the boardroom and dining room by a new toplit staircase formed of steel and timber. Individual offices have been designed for the directors, including a pavilion-like extension on to an existing roof terrace. The calm space provides a setting for art works and specially chosen furnishings.

Pilcher Hershman Also part of the refurbishment of 25 Savile Row, the offices designed by Squire and Partners for Pilcher Hershman reflect the strong taste of the clients, who sought to express the character of their operations in the fit-out. The design

concept is based on a series of increasingly private spaces leading from a striking gallery to the reception and open plan offices, ending in bespoke directors' offices leading to a roof terrace. Materials used include limestone, walnut and white marble.

Price and Myers For engineers, Price and Myers, with whom Squire and Partners have collaborated professionally on a number of projects, the practice designed new offices in a recently refurbished five storey block in Newman Street, W1. The client wished to create offices with a strong image but equally conducive to social interaction and highly efficient working for professional staff. The reception area on to Newman Street, forms a "shopfront" for the firm and is visually connected to the offices beyond, where the desking is placed to the perimeter. Dining, library and meeting spaces are at basement level. The calm ambience of the offices is reinforced by a carefully chosen palette of materials.

Squire and Partners The practice's own offices at 77 Wicklow Street are designed to cater for the needs of a rapidly growing company. The ground and lower ground floors of a former printing works were designed to encourage communication and interaction in an open and attractive environment. Voids in the new floor slab unite the two floor levels, which are connected by two elegant staircases made of pre-cast concrete steps on a concrete spine, and channel daylight into the lower level. The ground floor reception area is connected to the cafe and meeting rooms by a gently ramped glass bridge, with views down into the space where the office's weekly project meetings take place. Informal meeting areas are provided adjacent to the main working spaces.

1 Park Place
Canary Wharf, London E14

1 Park Place is a new 25,000 sqm office building located on West India Avenue on the main axis to Cabot Square, the principal space at Canary Wharf, and is designed within the overall guidelines for the Canary Wharf estate. Externally, Portland stone and glass are the dominant materials.

It is a state-of-the-art commercial building, highly serviced and designed to meet the needs of international business with open plan dealer floors at lower levels and atriums providing natural light to offices at upper levels, where typical floor plates are 2,800 sqm.

The building has a strong urban presence, with a double-height recessed arcade at street level. The main entrance frames a striking view to West India Dock, with the dramatic central atrium separating the two sections of the building (connected by upper level bridges). A dockside walkway is planned to connect with the existing Canary Wharf walkway.

The facade is informed by the masterplan design guidelines, and the building sits comfortably on West India Avenue

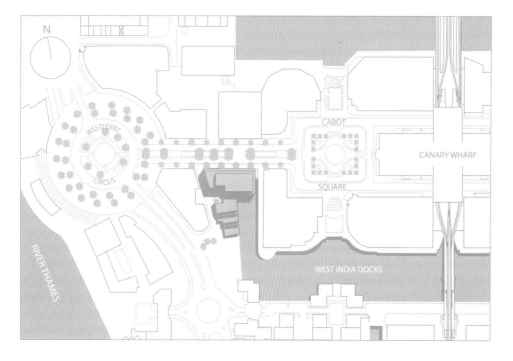

Client
Grenadier Investments Ltd
Contract Value
£40m
Quantity Surveyor
E C Harris
Structural Engineer
Whitby Bird and Partners
Services Engineer
BDSP Partnership
Planning Consent
2001

Parnell House
25 Wilton Road, London SW1

The site for the Parnell House scheme was highly prominent: close to Victoria Station, with the listed Apollo Theatre next door. The existing building on the site had frontages to both Wilton Road and Vauxhall Bridge Road. Refurbishment of this structure was ruled out after its condition was found to be poor, with extensive corrosion of the steel frame.

The redevelopment of the site focuses on a transverse atrium, connecting the two frontages of the building, which forms an internal "street" and reception area and contains the main circulation routes, including the main lifts (contained in translucent glazed shafts). Two large open-plan floor plates at each level are separated by the atrium (clad in light stone), which channels daylight into the working areas. The use of post-tensioned slabs allows the office floors to be column-free. Each of the plates has its own cores, set against party walls at the edges of the site, so that they can be let separately. The offices are designed for maximum flexibility and are provided with raised floors, demountable suspended ceilings and full VAV air conditioning.

The strong diagram of the building is matched by a rigorous elevational treatment which frankly expresses the structural frame while respecting the established context – Portland stone is the predominant material, with the base of the building faced in salmon pink flame-textured granite. The building contains around 7,500 sqm of lettable office space with some retail space at street level and four flats on the 6th floor.

The 'glazed street' connecting the two principal facades provides entrances, and lets light into the deep plan

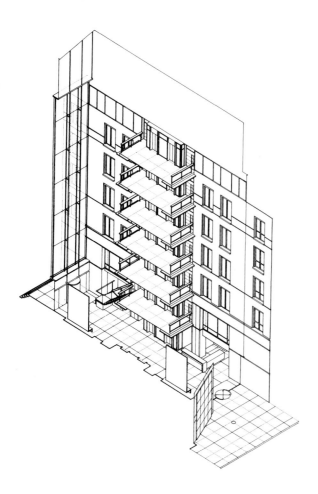

Client
CIS Ltd
Contract Value
£14m
Project Manager
John Shreeves and Partners
Quantity Surveyor
John Shreeves and Partners
Structural Engineer
Richard Watkins and Associates
Services Engineer
M&E Design Services
Main Contractor
Alfred McAlpine
Completed
1997

The atrium is generously
lit by glass walls at
either end

21–23 Red Lion Street
London WC1

The 21–23 Red Lion Street project was an exercise in transformation. The existing building was an unremarkable 1950s block, which Squire and Partners converted into 14 apartments.

The flats are arranged on seven floors, with duplex units on ground and basement level and on the 4th and 5th floors – all other apartments are on one level. The existing set-back at 3rd floor level was replaced by additional accommodation and new penthouses added at roof level – these contain double-height living areas with mezzanine levels opening on to a timber-decked roof terrace. The setting back of the ground floor allows natural light into basement areas.

The external language of the block is straightforward and urbane, with a new rendered elevation. Oak boarding and metal railings are used to modify the scale of the new windows and oak is also used at the entrances to the maisonettes, with panels linking entrance doors and window bays.

The existing building is extended to provide new accommodation at high level, while the ground floor is cut away to allow light to the basement

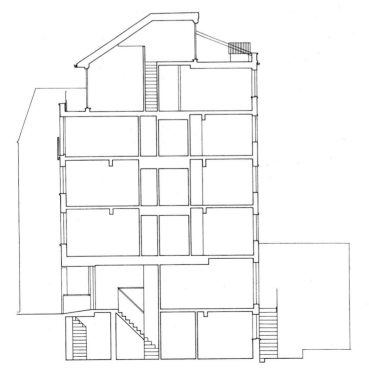

Client
Winyard Developments
Contract Value
£1.27m
Quantity Surveyor
Leonard Stace Partnership
Structural Engineer
David Jones
Main Contractor
Marldon
Completed
1998

The interiors are
articulated by separating
new partitions from
existing structural walls
which are carved out to
create sculptural openings

Residential

Squire and Partners' portfolio of residential projects is extremely varied, responding to the specific circumstances of very diverse locales. These may range from well-established and prestigious residential quarters to former industrial areas where factories and warehouses are being recycled as housing. The practice is well known for its vigorous response to riverside and other waterfront sites. All the practice's projects reflect a deeply held conviction about the appropriateness of contemporary design in historic contexts.

9 Abbey Road
A development of 21 new apartments completed in 2002 (replacing a nondescript car showroom) providing a strikingly contemporary addition to St John's Wood. The double-skin facade features a glazed outer skin, providing enclosed balconies and giving the building a sleek appearance by day or night. The glazed facade is flanked by Portland stone clad "bookend" wings, which provide a visual link to adjacent buildings. To the rear, white glazed bricks are used, providing a clean and simple look in keeping with the surroundings.
Client Persimmon Homes (South East) Ltd

491–493 Liverpool Road
Located in a Conservation Area, this scheme involves the conversion of former industrial buildings and a new build development of 14 apartments and houses on the site of demolished sheds. The existing building fronting on to Liverpool Road is modified with a new entrance area and the existing brickwork cleaned and repaired. A basement area excavated between the pavement and the building facade allows natural light to permeate lower floors. The new building facing Paradise Park includes a four-storey block of nine apartments plus five terraced houses. Extensive glazing and balconies capitalise on views to the park.
Client Winyard Developments

121–125 Edgware Road
The character of Edgware Road is partly defined by the run of inter-war apartment blocks extending along its west side – typically these are steel-framed structures faced in brick and Portland stone. Squire and Partners' designs for 19 apartments, plus retailing and basement parking space, takes its cue from this established context, while providing a high quality modern addition to the streetscape. The development rises to eight storeys on the corner of Burwood Place, with a double height glazed rooftop pavillion housing two superb penthouses. The buliding sweeps down to three storeys on its side elevation.
Client Persimmon Homes (South East) Ltd

Old Swan Wharf is a riverside development of 14 apartments on a site next to Battersea Old Church. All the flats enjoy fine views of the Thames. The riverside elevation of the scheme is relatively formal, while that to the narrow Church Road is a simple brick screen, following the line of the street. The scheme incorporates a new riverside walkway, connecting to the existing walkway, and a small public square and slipway, linking the development visually to the churchyard.
Client St George Developments Ltd

Royal Victoria Docks Masterplan
London E14

Squire and Partners were responsible for the masterplanning of the area to the west of the ExCeL exhibition centre at Royal Victoria Dock. The Masterplan incorporates a wide range of uses which will animate the connections between the DLR stations and the dock, as well as the axial approach to the exhibition centre, which runs parallel to the quayside.

The Masterplan is generated from a series of urban forms and spaces layered behind the principal buildings on the edge of the dock. Retail and restaurant uses animate the ground floor, with residential hotel and business uses supporting the exhibition centre. The principal buildings set on the dock edge refer to the original robust warehouse buildings, which were connected to the quayside mooring points.

A new bridge link and pedestrian connection from the Royal Victoria DLR station follows the orientation set up in the existing landscaping adjoining ExCeL and the Thames Barrier Park. Towers marking the key locations within the site provide spectacular views of Canary Wharf and the Millennium Dome.

The robust massing on the edge of the dock responds to the organisation of the original warehouses

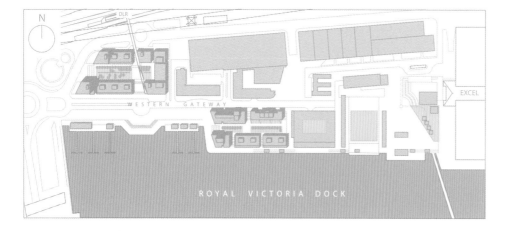

Client
Marylebone Warwick
Balfour Group
plc/Milequay Ltd
Contract Value
£100m
Planning Consent
2001

St Andrew's Church
Short Street, London SE1

Squire and Partners' development for the parish of Waterloo and the Manhattan Loft Corporation combines new church and community facilities with commercial units and residential apartments. The scheme replaces a 1950s church, unlisted and in poor condition, which is no longer viable for the needs of the parish.

The designs provide for a linked group of buildings in which the church/community and commercial developments are conceived as distinctive elements. The church building addresses the corner of Short Street and Ufford Street and is constructed of curving brickwork and white render, with translucent glazing to express the volumes within – two stacked halls, intended for use by local arts and community groups as well as by the parish, which overlook an enclosed garden to the rear.

The residential development has its own entrance via a full-height, four storey reception lobby. The apartments enjoy floor to ceiling glazing in living areas – bedrooms are set back behind balconies for greater privacy. The mix of materials on the apartments – render, brickwork, translucent and transparent glass – provides a crisply layered facade to the street. This scheme is a significant contribution to the regeneration of the South Bank.

The new church responds to its corner location and will be luminous at night

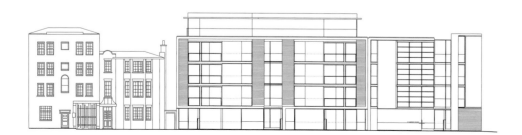

Client
Manhattan Loft Corporation
Contract Value
£2.6m
Quantity Surveyor
Tropus
Structural Engineer
Alan Baxter Associates
Services Engineer
Optima
Planning Consent
2002

74 St James's Street
London SW1

Squire & Partners' £40 million office project at 74 St James's Street involves the restoration and conversion of a Grade II* listed Victorian clubhouse with a new 11,500 sqm building along Little St James's Street to the rear, connected by a glazed atrium, replacing existing buildings of the 1950s and 60s.

Original features and finishes within the 1840 former Conservative Club will be carefully restored on the basis of extensive research and in consultation with English Heritage. The design of the new building is an exercise in marrying Classical scale and symmetry with contemporary detailing. It will be clad in limestone with simple aluminium framed windows punctuating the facade. The full-height glazed atrium, rising five floors, will provide a clear transition from listed building to new development and contains the main circulation for the entire scheme.

The scheme enriches the surrounding Conservation Area, providing an assured future for the listed building while adding an element of sensitive modern design.

The new building on Little St James's Street responds to the materials and character of the area

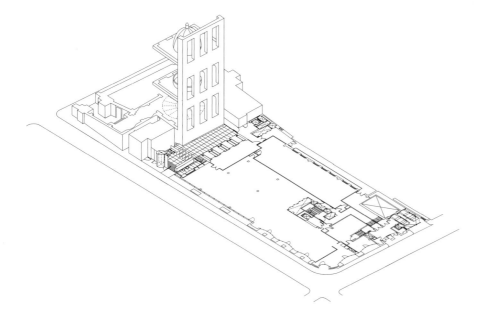

Client
Chelworth Holdings Ltd
Contract Value
£47m
Project Manager
Delta Property Services Ltd
Quantity Surveyor
E C Harris
Structural Engineer
Waterman
Partnership/Alan Baxter
and Associates
Services Engineer
Interserve
Main Contractor
Kajima
Completion
2003

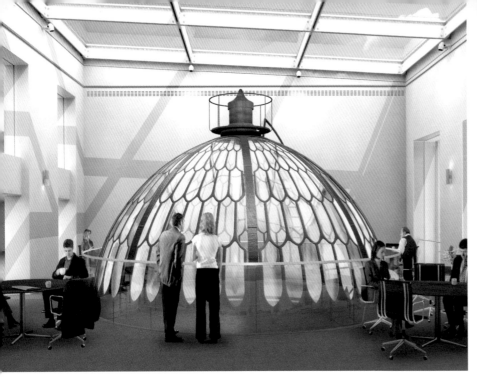

The relationship between
the new and existing
elements of the building
create a dynamic which
is complementary to
them both

Sand Bar and Restaurant

156 Clapham Park Road, London SW4

The Sand bar and restaurant project has transformed a rundown pub in Clapham, south London, into a high quality venue. The existing pub had a cramped and inconvenient layout. The reconstruction has provided a series of intimate spaces at ground floor level, with half the area raised to provide better headroom for WCs now located in the basement. The seating areas are defined by a series of low walls and screens – slit openings in these divisions allow views across the bar. They are also used to expose and illuminate the perimeter brick walls and to display objects. The inventiveness of the project extends to the WCs, with their unisex handwashing area, dominated by a long timber trough backed by five black enamelled wash stations, the whole strikingly lit.

The predominant material in the bar is natural, unpainted sand cement render, with concealed lighting used to produce a sympathetic warm glow. The bar top is of pure, dyed resin panels on a steel structure with lighting beneath and a dark brown leather front. Fixed furniture consists of deep stained timber bench seats. In total, nearly 280 sqm of space was refurbished at basement, ground and first floor levels – the first floor is designed as a private members' club.

The bar is clad in leather, with a stainless steel plinth and an illuminated resin top

Client
Sand Bar Ltd
Contract Value
£0.45m
Quantity Surveyor
E C Harris
Structural Engineer
Price and Myers
Main Contractor
Cirus Ltd
Completed
1999

The bar/restaurant is designed as a series of intimate spaces which 'evolve' during the course of an evening

25 Savile Row
London W1

The £1.33 million refurbishment of 25 Savile Row, a 5 storey 1950s office building, has produced new office space of exceptional quality and enhanced the public domain. The project was carried out for Derwent Valley Holdings plc and includes the design of the clients' own office, which was relocated from Wimpole Street, as well as the refitting of the reception area and lifts. The project benefited from close consultation with the client, a reflection of the long experience of collaboration between Derwent Valley and Squire and Partners. The aim was to create a strong and distinct identity for the building, reflecting Derwent Valley's reputation for commissioning high quality contemporary design.

The refurbished reception area is a key element in the scheme and is conceived as an open and inviting "shop front" to the building with a strong presence on the street. The facade was brought out to the original building line with large glazing panels wrapping around the corner to Boyle Street and allowing the whole area to be clearly seen from the pavement. The simple entrance canopy is set with fibre optic lighting. Inside, a limited palette of fine materials has been used with dramatic effect. The reception desk is faced with a single piece of white veined marble, 3m x 1.1m. It is framed by the curved leather wall behind, developed in collaboration with designer Bill Amberg and reflecting the tailoring traditions of Savile Row. Flooring is of limestone slabs, 1m square.

The 'street level' allows transparency and interaction between the architecture and the inhabitants of the city

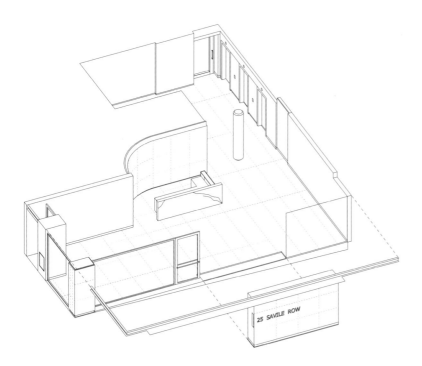

25 SAVILE ROW

Client
Derwent Valley
Holdings plc
Contract Value
£1.33m
Quantity Surveyor
Davis Langdon and Everest
Structural Engineer
Price and Myers
Services Engineer
Peter Deer and
Associates
Main Contractor
Sames plc
Completed
2000

The new 'sky storey' addresses the city as a whole, defining its skyline and its profile

111 Strand
London W1

The office development at 111 Strand is located on one of London's principal thoroughfares, close to the Savoy Hotel. The corner site, formerly occupied by undistinguished late 19th and 20th century buildings, backs on to a tranquil area of gardens around the ancient Savoy Chapel. While sensitive to its context, the new 2700 sqm, six storey office building is uncompromisingly modern in appearance – strongly modelled, its external facades feature limestone panels set in metal frames with curved bays of Portland stone and glass to emphasise the junction of the Strand with the narrow Savoy Street, which leads to the Embankment.

With the support of the client, Patrick Despard of City and West End Developments, Squire and Partners are working with artists Langlands & Bell on a major artwork for the building. This will occupy an area of the Strand facade adjacent to the main entrance and will consist of a stone relief depicting the area of cityscape around the building. Visitors and passers-by will find the city upturned and re-presented as a view from above on the facade.

The facade responds
to the rhythms and
fabric of the adjoining
buildings

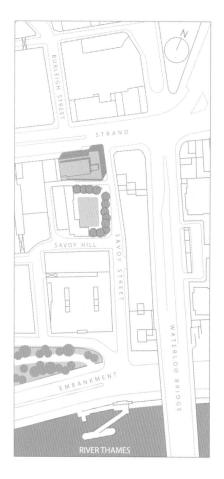

Client
City and West End
Developments
Contract Value
£8.8m
Quantity Surveyor
E C Harris/Mott Green Wall
Structural Engineer
Campbell Reith Hill
Services Engineer
Mecserve
Main Contractor
Kier London
Completed
2002

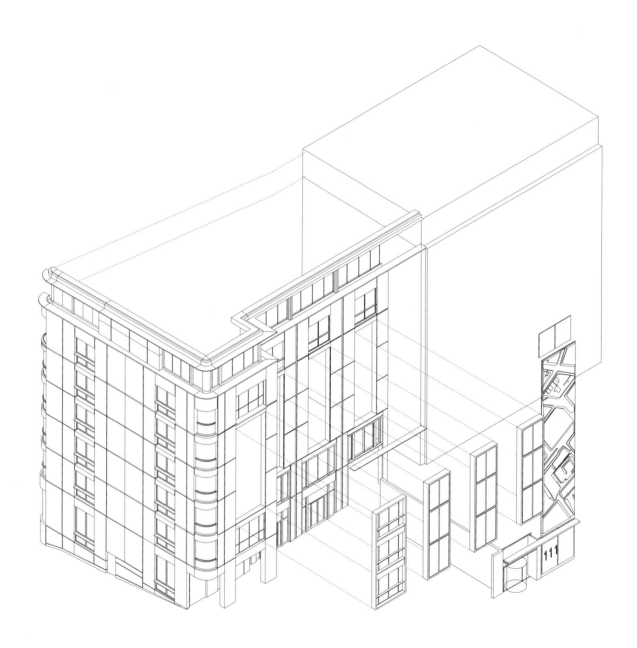

A Portland stone sculpture
panel has been designed
for the building by
Langlands & Bell.
The panel is a graphic
depiction of the local
area in relief

Sufferance Wharf
London E14

In this scheme, completed in 1990, Squire and Partners established a new vernacular for housing in the revived Docklands. The site is on the Isle of Dogs, between West Ferry Road and the river, close to Canary Wharf.

The development of high quality apartments and houses takes its cue, in terms of scale, form and materials, from the traditional warehouse architecture of the Docklands. Yellow brick is used as the main cladding material, combined with white render, light steelwork and areas of glazing. The layout of the scheme seeks to reflect the historic urban form of the area, with its streets and squares. The main riverside block contains 67 flats and six two-storey rooftop penthouses plus health club and swimming pool at ground level – a two storey base gives scale to the building. Behind are nine mews houses and 41 apartments in lower blocks enclosing a landscaped courtyard. The access to the development is via a new street between the courtyard block and the mews houses. This street terminates at the glazed, two storey reception. The glazing allows a view from West Ferry Road to the river.

The building is supported over the public riverside walkway by a 'forest' of slender white columns

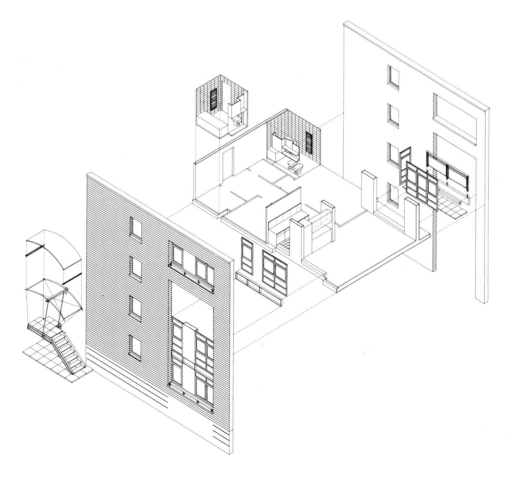

Client
Rosehaugh Copartnership
Developments Ltd
Contract Value
£17.2m
Project Manager
John Shreeves and
Partners
Quantity Surveyor
E C Harris
Structural Engineer
Cooper Macdonald and
Partners
Services Engineer
M&E Design Services
Main Contractor
Costain Construction
Completed
1990

The new building
responds to the
original robust
riverside warehouses

Tower Bridge Visitor Facilities
London EC3

Completed in 1894, Tower Bridge is one of London's most familiar landmarks, combining engineering virtuosity with exuberant architectural form, and is a Grade I listed World Heritage site. Squire and Partners was commissioned to design new visitor facilities for the Bridge, to be completed to mark its centenary in 1994. The new entrance building and ticket office, a simple structure of painted steel infilled with cladding panels of glass and terrazzo, stands on one of the main piers. Its lightweight, airy aesthetic provides a striking contrast to the monumentality of the Bridge.

The curved form of the new building follows the profile of the existing pier. It is designed to provide both a place for visitors to queue for admission and a clear route for pedestrians crossing the Bridge.

The delicate structure touches Tower Bridge lightly while it responds to the geometry of the cutwater

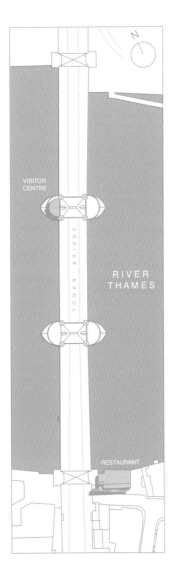

VISITOR
CENTRE

TOWER BRIDGE

RIVER
THAMES

RESTAURANT

Client
Corporation of London
Contract Value
£0.25m
Project Manager
Bowes Darby
Quantity Surveyor
Frost Bevan
Structural Engineer
Whitby Bird and Partners
Main Contractor
John Mowlem
Construction
Completed
1993

Tower Bridge Restaurant
Portland Wharf, London SE1

The project for a restaurant at Portland Wharf, at the south end of Tower Bridge, echoes the lightweight, minimal approach taken by Squire and Partners in the design of the visitor facilities for the bridge. The new building forms an elegant counterpoise to the ornate bulk of the Victorian structure. By placing the restaurant on two levels, with a bar at the lower level, public access to the riverside is continued, with a new square providing excellent views of the bridge and the river. The restaurant itself is canted out to make best use of views along the Thames.

The restaurant is conceived as a simple glazed box, with frameless glazing in a solid stone frame, hung off the flight of stone stairs which runs down from bridge level and provides a much improved pedestrian access to the Butler's Wharf area.

The new building incorporates public steps leading from Tower Bridge to Shad Thames

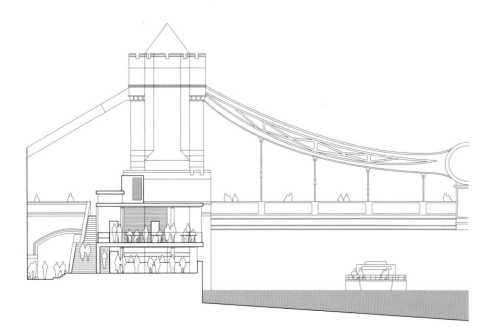

Client
Corporation of London
Contract Value
£2m
Structural Engineer
Whitby Bird and Partners
Services Engineer
Whitby Bird and Partners
Planning consent
2000

Vogans Mill
Mill Street, London SE1

The Vogan's Mill project in Bermondsey, completed in 1989, became a symbol of regeneration in London Docklands, not least because it reused an apparently problematic industrial structure, a redundant grain silo. The robustly-built silo, sited in a Conservation Area, was reconstructed on the existing concrete frame as a 17 storey residential tower, with one apartment per floor. On top, a new lightweight structure contains a spectacular three-storey penthouse with fine views across the South Bank, the river and the City of London.

The success of the scheme as an exercise in practical conservation was recognised by awards from the Civic Trust and RTPI. The tower, previously hardly noticed, became the setting for a number of films and television commercials, with the penthouse selling for a price previously unheard of in the area.

The adjacent listed Victorian warehouses, facing on to St Saviour's Dock, were converted to 48 apartments, with a new link block on the dockside. The architectural form of this striking intervention is deliberately lightweight and entirely contemporary, using a cladding of metal and glass, but refers subtly to the industrial traditions of the area.

The new quayside buildings reinforce the retained listed warehouses

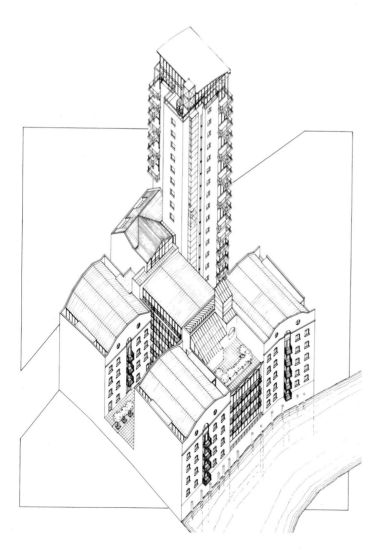

Client
Rosehaugh Copartnership
Developments Ltd
Contract Value
£10m
Project Manager
John Shreeves and
Partners
Quantity Surveyor
E C Harris
Structural Engineer
Cooper Macdonald and
Partners
Services Engineer
M&E Design Services
Main Contractor
John Lelliott (Contracts)
Completed
1989

The original concrete grain
silo is reconstructed to
provide spectacular
new residential
accommodation

London's West End has long been a focus for Squire and Partners' work. It is an urban territory of dramatic contrasts – from the major shopping thoroughfares of Oxford Street, Regent Street, Piccadilly and Bond Street to the small-scale variety of Soho. But the roots of the West End lie in the 18th century when Mayfair and Marylebone were laid out by great landowners. In the Regency period, John Nash's civic improvements gave London a dignity it had previously lacked. Squire and Partners' work in the West End responds to its underlying order and explicit architectural rhythm while seeking a way to express those qualities in a contemporary manner.

Brewer Street Proposals for a new-mixed use development in Soho replace an existing NCP car park, a large 1930s structure completely filling a block between Brewer Street, Lexington Street, Peter Street and Ingestre Place and forming an impenetrable intervention in the historic landscape. It is proposed that the car parking is relocated on six underground levels and the site at ground level contains an office building on Brewer Street accessed from a striking glazed pavilion set on the axis of Great Windmill Street and replacing the existing solid tower. The Brewer Street frontage is given over to retail units and the residential development will be approached from a new public space at the end of Peter Street.
Client NCP/Helical Bar

Chesham House This substantial block backs onto Warwick Street, Soho, but also forms part of the sequence of imposing, stone-fronted facades of Regent Street. The existing building, Grade II listed, contains poor quality offices which are to be radically upgraded as part of the Crown Estate's Vision Strategy for Regent Street. The listed Regent Street facade remains largely unchanged. Behind the facade, the existing structure is replaced by a new development with retailing at basement, ground and first floor levels and high quality offices above. The major design challenge in the scheme was the creation of a new frontage on Warwick Street, replacing the present utilitarian facade.
Client The Crown Estate

40-42 Portman Square
Two 1950s buildings are to be demolished for a new £30m headquarters and luxury residential building. The site is in one of London's most prestigious squares. Seven floors of office space are proposed, plus two floors of serviced apartments and penthouses – set back from the main building line and expressed as glazed pavilions. The main north-facing facade balances solid and glazed elements. On the south side, facing a mews, brick and limestone panels with solar shading baffle the sun as well as reflecting the more informal character of the mews.
Client Delancey Estates plc

4-6 Savile Row Squire and Partners has obtained planning permission to replace an existing 1960s block with a new office and retail development. The site is within the Mayfair Conservation Area and a high quality new building was required. The facade responds to the established context with a clear division into base, middle storeys and attic/sky storey. There are five floors of offices, including the lightweight pent-house floor. Portland stone is used to express the structural frame, with inset bronze panels.
Client Benchmark Group plc

West India Quay Masterplan
London E14

Squire and Partners' masterplan for West India Quay addressed a number of issues; the creation of a leisure and residential quarter to complement the major office developments at nearby Canary Wharf, the conversion of redundant Grade I listed warehouses (the best surviving in Docklands), the design of appropriate landscaping, and the insulation of the site against noise from the Limehouse Link road and Docklands Light Railway, which run just to the north of the masterplan site.

The site was the subject of a 1996 competition run by the LDDC and won by the West India Quay Development Company consortium with Squire and Partners as architects. The aim was to provide facilities which served not just the immediate area but equally the wider local community.

The masterplan provided for the conversion of the warehouses to apartments, plus 8000 sqm of retail and restaurant use at quayside level. Behind the warehouses, a new 10 screen multiplex cinema complex and multi storey car park for 800 cars provide a baffle against road and railway. Consent was obtained for a new 32 storey tower, housing apartments and a hotel.

The new glass tower sits on the axis of the quayside and the Limehouse Link Road which connects the Isle of Dogs to the City

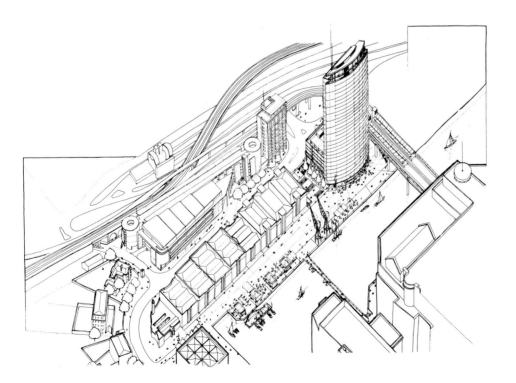

Client
West India Quay
Development Company
Contract Value
£90m
Project Manager
E C Harris/MDA Group UK
Quantity Surveyor
E C Harris/MDA Group UK
Structural Engineer
Waterman Partnership
Services Engineer Northern Site
M&E Design Services
Services Engineer Eastern Site
Flack and Kurtz (UK) Ltd
Architect for Warehouses
FSP Architects
Planning consent
1997

The new Future Systems
floating pedestrian bridge
connects the development
to Canary Wharf

West India Quay Multiplex
London E14

The site north of the listed West India Quay warehouses, on Hertsmere Road, has been developed to provide a 10 screen, 2100 seat multiplex cinema, with ancillary retailing, and a health club.

The multiplex is linked to the new shops, bars and restaurants on the quayside, the whole forming a major addition to the leisure provision in Docklands and serving local residents and Canary Wharf workers. The glazed wall of the multiplex is designed as an organising element leading pedestrians into the site.

The new multiplex cinema addresses the new public open space

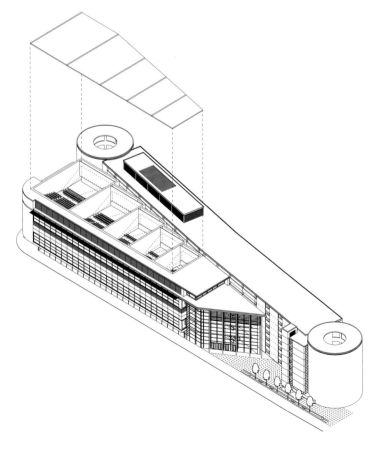

Client
West India Quay
Development Company
Contract Value
£14.5m
Project Manager
E C Harris/MDA Group UK
Quantity Surveyor
E C Harris/MDA Group UK
Structural Engineer
Waterman Partnership
Services Engineer
M&E Design Services
Main Contractor
Lovell Construction
Completed
2000

Circulation is set on the outside of the building to provide animation

West India Quay Landscaping
London E14

Public space is a vital element in the regeneration of West India Quay for which the Squire and Partners' masterplan forms a framework. Two landscaped squares have been formed, one along the waterside, the other adjacent to the multiplex cinema and multistorey carpark. The aim is to blur the interface between "public" and "private" domains and create a lively environment.

The restaurants and cafes in the renovated warehouses animate the south-facing quayside

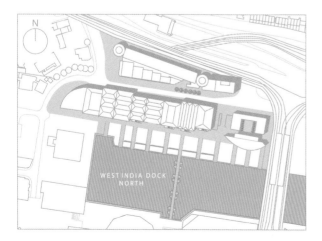

Client
West India Quay
Development Company
Contract Value
£1.2m
Project Manager
E C Harris/MDA Group UK
Quantity Surveyor
E C Harris/MDA Group UK
Structural Engineer
Waterman Partnership
Services Engineer
M&E Design Services
Main Contractor
Lovell Construction
Completed
2000

CLIENTS

Alan Baxter Associates
The Apperly Estates Ltd
Asticus (UK) Ltd
Ballymore Properties
Barratt (East London) Ltd
Beaumont Property Consulting
Benchmark Group plc
Berkeley Homes Ltd
Bilfinger + Berger Development UK
Boultbee Land plc
The Brand Union
The Brighton West Pier Trust
British Council
Brook House Developments Ltd
Central & City
Central & Metropolitan
Cheval Property Management Ltd
CIS Ltd
CityWell
City & West End
Clerical and Medical Investment Group
Colebrook Estates
Compass Partners International
Comshare Ltd
Corporation of London
Corob Holdings Ltd
Crest Nicholson
The Crown Estate
Delancey Estates plc
Delta Property Services
Derwent Valley Holdings plc
Development Securities plc
Dorrington Investments
Dresdner Private Banking
Duchy of Lancaster
Ebble Trading Ltd
Euronav (UK) Agencies Ltd
Fairclough Homes
Grafton Estates plc
Grainger Trust plc

Grenadier Investments Ltd
Grosvenor
Helical Bar
Henderson Property Asset Management
Hightown Holdings Ltd
Holmes Place
HSBC Investment Bank plc
The Hurlingham Club
JER Real Estate Advisors
King's Fund
199 Knightsbridge Developments Ltd
Ladymead Investments
Limehouse Youth Club
London Borough of Tower Hamlets
London Docklands Development Corporation
London & Amsterdam Properties
London & Hereford Holdings Ltd
London Merchant Securities Ltd
London & Metropolitan Estates Ltd
London & Quadrant Housing Trust
London Underwriting Centre
Lonrho plc
Manhattan Loft Corporation
Marylebone Warwick Balfour Group plc
MEPC Developments Ltd
Milequay Ltd
Millard Properties Ltd
National Car Parks
NHP Developments Ltd
Pace Investments
Park Estates Southern Ltd
P&O Developments Ltd
Persimmon Homes (SE) Ltd
Pilcher Hershman
Precis Property
Price and Myers
The Private Property & Investment Company
Redrow Commercial Developments
Rosehaugh Copartnership Developments
Royal Bank of Scotland

Rugby Estates plc
St Bartholomew's Medical College
St George plc
St James Homes
St Martin's Property Corporation Ltd
Sainsbury's
Sand Bar Ltd
Shell UK Ltd
Paul Stevens Properties Ltd
Stockham Investments
Sunley Holdings plc
Taylor Woodrow Capital Developments
UGC Cinemas
Victoria and Albert Museum
Warden Housing Association
Warnford Investments
Wembley Stadium Ltd
West India Quay Development Company
Winyard Developments Ltd

AWARDS AND EXHIBITIONS

Awards

2002, British Council for Offices Award
  77 Wicklow Street
2002, Camden Design Award
  77 Wicklow Street
2001, Timber Industry Awards
  40 Portman Square Reception
2001, The Times/Gestetner Digital
  Office Collection
  25 Savile Row
2001 British Council for Offices Award
  25 Savile Row
2001 NAS Design Partnership Award
  25 Savile Row
2001 FX Interior Design Awards
  25 Savile Row
2000, The Times/Gestetner Digital
  Office Collection
  8 Cromwell Place, The Brand Union
2000, IAS/OAS
  Development of the Year Awards,
  4 Bouverie Street
2000, Civic Trust Awards
  51–53 Marlborough Hill
2000, MIPIM Awards
  Brook House
1998, Brick Awards
  Best Housing Development
  Brook House
1998, RIBA Housing Project Award
  West India Quay
1997, Evening Standard New Homes Awards
  Best New Apartment
  Chinnocks Wharf
1995, What Housing Awards
  Best Exterior, Old Swan Wharf
1994, RIBA Housing Project Award
  Old Swan Wharf
1993, Civic Trust Award,
  Vogans Mill

Exhibitions

2002, RIBA
  Housing Design
  16–32 Whitechurch Lane
2002, RIBA
  Neighbourhoods by Design
  West India Quay
2001, RIBA
  Housing Design
  Liverpool Road
1999, RIBA
  Space
  21–23 Red Lion Street
1999, RIBA
  Eating Design
  Sand bar and restaurant
1998, RIBA
  Working Design
  4 Grosvenor Place
1997, RIBA
  How did they do that?
  Limehouse Youth Club

BIBLIOGRAPHY

2002 July, The Architects' Journal
    Technical Feature, 111 Strand
2002 February, The Architects' Journal
    Good Practice, 77 Wicklow Street
2001 May, FX
    Tailor-made, 25 Savile Row,
    6 Greencoat Place, Greencoat House
2000 October, Property Week
    Turning New Corners, 4 Bouverie Street
2000 March, Architecture Today
    *Facade and Frame: Michael Squire
    and Partners in London*, 10 Lower
    Grosvenor Place, 4 Bouverie Street
2000 February/March, Building
    Design Interiors
    Just Deserts, Sand
1999 November 25, The Architects' Journal
    Dramatic Entrances, 90 Long Acre,
    101 Finsbury Pavement
1998 October 15, The Architects' Journal
    Rooms with a View, Brook House
1998 June, RIBA Journal
    Flat Top, 4 Grosvenor Place 6th Floor
1997 Dec, RIBA Interiors
    Making an Entrance, Greencoat House,
    4 Grosvenor Place, 10 Dean Farrar Street
1997 January 24, Building Design
    Just the Tonic for Docklands,
    West India Quay
1997 October, Architecture Today
    Double Aspect in Victoria, Parnell House
1996 February 22, The Architects' Journal
    *A Practice Where Design Begins at
    the Office*, 8 Cromwell Place
1996 February 22, The Architects' Journal
    New Focus for Docklands Youth,
    Limehouse Youth Club
1996 February 22, The Architects' Journal
    People, Michael Squire Associates
1996 February, Architecture Today

Down to Earth, 4 Grosvenor Place
1996 February, RIBA Journal
    Building of the Month,
    Limehouse Youth Club
1994 March, RIBA Journal
    Thick Skinned, Tower Bridge Visitor Centre
1992 November 27, Building Design
    Tower Exhibit, Tower Bridge Exhibition
1992 March 27, Building Design
    Inside Outing, 112-120 Brompton Road
1991 September 4, The Architects' Journal
    Museum Shortlist, Museum of Scotland
1990 November 30, Building Design
    Class Wharf, Sufferance Wharf
1990 May 16, The Architects' Journal
    Current Account, Vogans Mill
1990 March 16, Building Design
    An Urban Identity, Practice Profile
1989 November, Refurbishment
    Mix and Match, Vogans Mill

PROJECT INDEX

CATEGORY INDEX

CREDITS

Photographs
Philip Bier
BRD Associates
Richard Cheatle
Peter Cook
Christopher Edgcombe
Christopher Gascoigne
Nicholas Kane
Benedict Luxmoore
James Morris
Henrietta Van den Bergh
Morley von Sternberg
Charlotte Wood

Computer generated images
Smoothe
Miller Hare
Stephen Davis
Threedi

Artists
Langlands & Bell (Belgrave House and 111 Strand)

Design
Thomas Manss & Company

Copywriting
Ken Powell

©2002 Squire and Partners

Published by Squire and Partners
77 Wicklow Street London WC1X 9JY
Tel 020 7278 5555   Fax 020 7239 0495
pr@squireandpartners.com
www.squireandpartners.com

ISBN 0-9543441-0-3
Printed in the UK